WHO STOLE THE SECRET
TO THE
INDUSTRIAL
REVOLUTION?

Dedicated to the Italian and English engineers and inventors of the second millennium AD for their hard work and development of textile manufacturing machinery, especially for automation of spinning procedures, which were of so much benefit to the silk industry in Italy and to both the silk and cotton industries in England. A special dedication to a former curator of Quarry Bank Mill at Styal in Cheshire who first put the idea into my head that Richard Arkwright did not invent the water frame.

WHO STOLE THE SECRET
TO THE
INDUSTRIAL REVOLUTION?
THE REAL STORY BEHIND RICHARD ARKWRIGHT AND THE WATER FRAME

Glynis Cooper

PEN & SWORD
HISTORY

AN IMPRINT OF PEN & SWORD BOOKS LTD.
YORKSHIRE - PHILADELPHIA

First published in Great Britain in 2022 by
PEN AND SWORD HISTORY
An imprint of
Pen & Sword Books Ltd
Yorkshire – Philadelphia

ISBN 978 1 47387 591 3

A CIP catalogue record for this book is available from the British Library.

Typeset in Times New Roman 12/16 by SJmagic DESIGN SERVICES, India.
Printed and bound in the UK by CPI Group (UK) Ltd.

Pen & Sword Books Limited incorporates the imprints of Atlas, Archaeology,
Aviation, Discovery, Family History, Fiction, History, Maritime, Military,
Military Classics, Politics, Select, Transport, True Crime, Air World, Frontline
Publishing, Leo Cooper, Remember When, Seaforth Publishing, The Praetorian
Press, Wharncliffe Local History, Wharncliffe Transport, Wharncliffe True Crime
and White Owl.

For a complete list of Pen & Sword titles please contact
PEN & SWORD BOOKS LIMITED
47 Church Street, Barnsley, South Yorkshire, S70 2AS, England
E-mail: enquiries@pen-and-sword.co.uk
Website: www.pen-and-sword.co.uk

Or
PEN AND SWORD BOOKS
1950 Lawrence Rd, Havertown, PA 19083, USA
E-mail: Uspen-and-sword@casematepublishers.com
Website: www.penandswordbooks.com

Contents

Foreword

The traditional view still held in Britain is that a Bolton wigmaker, Richard Arkwright, invented the water frame, a spinning frame powered by water, which was the key element of starting the Industrial Revolution in textile manufacture during the 1760s. He was also credited with being 'the father of the factory system' because he built a powered cotton-spinning mill at Cromford in 1771.

He was honoured with a knighthood in his own lifetime, and he died a rich man. During the intervening centuries there have been books, exhibitions, commemorations of his achievements and he has been enshrined in school history syllabuses. There is nothing wrong with rewarding such contributions to England's industrial history except that Richard Arkwright never made them. This discovery was as shocking as it was profound, turning lifelong beliefs and assumptions upside down. It also begged the question of why such myths have been perpetuated, are still perpetuated in the age of the 'information super-highway' and remains officially deemed by the relevant authorities to be correct.

The real story has been well hidden and was only stumbled upon after a chance remark by a northern museum curator aroused curiosity. It has since proved to be a classic detective story which led from England's 'green and pleasant land' across the sea to Italy, to Tuscany, a region still full of medieval beauty and secrets. From Tuscany, the trail criss-crossed continents, leading back in history to the days of Marco Polo's adventures, the Crusades of the Knights Templar and further back still to the ancient Chinese civilisations of European pre-history. The Chinese had a secret which they managed to keep hidden for hundreds of years before sharing it with the rest of the world, an act which finally culminated in the Industrial Revolution and ultimately led to this book.

It may be regarded as 'unpatriotic' to detract from one's own country's technical prowess, but we are what our past has made us and if telling the truth is 'unpatriotic' then it ought not to be so. Britain rightfully takes the credit for numerous technological inventions and innovations too numerous to mention here. However, in this aspect of textile technology, Britain was not the prime mover. It was another country whose vital contribution has been practically airbrushed from history and its place in both British history and industrial history should be fully acknowledged.

To most British people, the term 'Industrial Revolution' means the eighteenth/nineteenth-century industrial revolution which, for a time, made Britain the centre of the world. It is often assumed that this was the first industrial revolution, but it wasn't. Far from it. It was simply the first industrial revolution to take place on English soil. Initially, the Chinese civilisations were technically far ahead of the West. In Antiquity, the Greeks, Romans and Sumerians laid the foundations of many modern-day discoveries. There have been industrial revolutions in Italy for the last thousand years, for much of which Italy was regarded as the leading technological country in Europe, but that fact seems to have faded into history. Italy has produced memorable numbers of talented artists, architects, craftsmen, inventors, sculptors and scientists over the centuries, as well as possibly the greatest mind of all time, that of Leonardo da Vinci. He was born 500 years ahead of his time, but he foresaw and invented so much that is still relevant today, and, like many other Italian craftsmen and scientists, he too has his part to play in this story.

Richard Arkwright, so far as is known, never travelled to Italy, but a number of his countrymen did, bringing back with them new ideas and experiences. A few, jealous of the wealth and success of

Italy, brought back things to which they had no right. Arkwright was a talented entrepreneur, good at sales and marketing and self-promotion, and he did play a part and make a contribution to the Industrial Revolution. However, he did not do what British history has given him the credit for doing. That belongs to other people. Somewhere along the way, Italy has lost its rightful place and credit for its part in the Industrial Revolution. The country's contribution to the revolution in textile manufacture has gone largely unrecorded and mostly unnoticed. A large number of Italian workers died during the Black Death of 1347–1349, the worst pandemic in recorded history. The loss of human labour prompted the growth of mechanical means to do the jobs that there were no longer enough people left to do. It was the Italians who led the way into the Industrial Revolution and their contribution should not be forgotten. The record needs to be set straight and credit given where credit is due.

Introduction

The term 'industrial revolution' is really a misnomer because it is referred to in the singular and it is generally assumed that there was only one Industrial Revolution, that which took place in Britain and western Europe during the eighteenth and nineteenth centuries. There have actually been a number of industrial revolutions over time across the world, but the most influential and long-lasting one occurred at an unknown date of pre-history in an unknown place when an unknown person first invented the wheel. Who invented the wheel, when and where, remains one of the major and most tantalising of historical scientific mysteries. The simple wheel has formed the basis of mechanics and engineering for thousands of years and had the innovation of that first wheel never been put into practice, our entire history would have been different, and the most well-known industrial revolution might never have happened.

The tale to be told here relies heavily on the use of the wheel in various aspects. The beginning of this story would make a good crossword clue: 'Connection between nineteenth-century cotton mills in Manchester and 7,000-year-old remote farming settlements in eastern China. Four letters.' The answer would be 'silk'. Early Chinese sericulture and the mechanised English textile manufacture of the Industrial Revolution were two worlds far apart in time and space which finally collided in the eighteenth century in ways that the prehistoric Chinese farmers could never have imagined. The historical records chronicle the unfolding of this story, but the oral tradition has always proved to be the most popular way of passing the details down the centuries, and, as in the well-known game of

Chinese Whispers, elements change, either through mishearing or misunderstanding, so that facts and statements become distorted, sometimes to the extent that they are just plain wrong. It happens in countries all over the world and perpetuates myths which are simply not true. This book is an attempt to correct one particular myth that has lasted over 250 years in Britain which falsifies an important part of British industrial history, thereby giving credit where credit is not due, and failing to acknowledge the part played by another country. The chief protagonists never met, being separated in the one case by decades and in the other cases by centuries. It is a story involving resentment, jealousy, power struggles, industrial espionage, love, betrayal, murder, revenge, and ending with the strangest of twists and the cruellest of ironies in a tale well worthy of the big screen.

Chapter 1

Brief History of Silk

Silk production first began *c.* 3000 BC (around the time the building of Stonehenge began) as a cottage industry of the Yangshuo culture in the small Neolithic farming villages along the Yellow River of Henan Province. The modern village of Yangshuo lies at the foot of the stunning conical peaks of the Loess Plateau just over 1,100 miles south of Beijing. Henan Province lies adjacent to Hebei Province and is one of the main sericulture (silk farming) areas of northern China. Early farmers made the best use of the resources around them and thus sericulture was born. Silkworms eat the leaves of mulberry trees, and a wide variety of mulberry trees, including white, red and black mulberry trees, grow in China. Different types are cultivated in different provinces. However, silkworms much prefer the leaves of the white mulberry trees. The English nursery rhyme, 'Here we go round the mulberry bush', first published during the 1840s, is said to celebrate mulberry trees and the English silk industry of the eighteenth and nineteenth centuries.

According to Strabo, the Greek word for 'silken' was *sericos*, from Seres, the people from whom the silk was first obtained. From the Greek word came the Latin *sericum* which translated as *sioloc* in Old English and was later modified to 'silk'. Silk is a fibre consisting of two proteins: fibroin and sericin. Fibroin forms the silk filament and sericin is a gum which binds the filaments together. A female silk moth can lay between 300 and 500 eggs from which silkworms hatch. After feeding on mulberry tree leaves until they have grown sufficiently, and, after moulting several times, the silkworms then spin a cocoon around themselves. This can take two or three days and involves about a mile of silk filament being secreted from salivary glands on the heads of the silkworms. When the cocoon is finished, the silkworms enclose themselves within it and it is at this point that the fine silken strands need to be unravelled. The live cocoons are therefore placed in boiling water which kills the enclosed pupae but softens the sericin gum so that the silk threads do not break. The silken threads, known as raw silk, are then wound on to a reel ready for weaving. There is growing concern in modern times that silk production is a cruel practice which causes unnecessary suffering. However, early Chinese farmers used cold water to soften the sericin and it is said that this gives the silk yarn extra lustre, and more brilliant colour when dyed.

The Chinese guarded the secrets of their silk manufacture jealously and the first Silk Road was strictly within the confines of the huge Chinese Empire. The opening up of trade routes beyond the Chinese Empire's borders coincided with the rise of the revered Chinese Han Dynasty (202 BC–AD 220) and did not happen until just a couple of centuries before the birth of Christ, 5,000 years after the establishment of silk production in China. Then the Silk Road became not just a single road, but a collection of trade routes connecting eastern Asia with southern Asia, India, Persia (which initially controlled the export of silk to Europe and Byzantium), Arabia, the Mediterranean countries and East Africa. Chang'an (in the west of Shaanxi Province, close to Luoyang, at the meeting of the Luo and Yellow Rivers in the west of Henan Province where the silk industry began) was the capital under the Western Han (206 BC–AD 220) and the Tang (618–907). By the time of the Tang Dynasty there were two main silk roads going south: one to the port of the Ganges on the Bay of Bengal and the other to what is now Myanmar (formerly Burma); while a third road led eastwards across the northern borders of Tibet crossing Iran (formerly Persia) into Syria which gave access to the Mediterranean and Byzantium. To the east of Bukhara in Uzbekistan, a road also branched south-east towards the Indian sub-continent but circled around the area now known as Pakistan. There were also sea routes from what today are Canton and Hanoi, with ships sailing round the area of south-east Asia (which currently includes Myanmar, Vietnam, Thailand (formerly Siam), Laos, and Cambodia)), eastwards across the Bay of Bengal, around the Indian sub-continent, from there north to Iran and then south-east round the Arabian peninsula and through the Red Sea to Egypt and north-west Africa. The major trading commodity of the Silk Road, as its name suggests, was indeed silk, but jade and gold, technological innovations, notably paper and gunpowder, as well as cultural exchanges, also made their way westwards together with less desirable commodities like plagues, of which the Black Death came to be the most feared and the most lethal.

After the collapse of the Roman Empire, Europe in general, and Italy in particular, slipped into a decline known as the Dark Ages. In AD 381 Ambrose, Bishop of Milan, put it succinctly by describing the towns of Italy as *semirutarum urbium cadavera* or 'the remains of half-ruined towns'. (Cipolla, Carlos M. 1976). Europe had entered a depression which lasted several centuries and was not helped by the early eighth-century invasion of southern Europe by the Muslims. Spain was first invaded by Muslims in 711 AD and over 1,300 years later their influences can still be seen and felt, especially in Andalucia. Carlos Cipolla, in his book *Before the Industrial Revolution* (1976), paints a picture of Dark Age Europe which sounds like a scene out of a Brothers Grimm fairy tale:

It was a poor and primitive Europe whose autocracy was in part both a cause and consequence of the decline of trade. Society was dominated by resignation, suspicion and fear. People withdrew into economic isolation of the manors, spiritual isolation in the monasteries, social and

3

political isolation in the feudal system … Arts, education, trade and production were reduced to minimal levels. … The population was small, production meagre, poverty extreme, social structures primitive … The prevailing values reflected a brutal and superstitious society.

Changes did not really appear until the time of the Crusades (1095–1204). However, Edith Ennen (1956) states there were 'three distinguishable areas in western Europe at this time: Italy, Spain and southern France; in which the towns, however impoverished, continued to exist throughout the Dark Ages … there was an essential continuity in the existence of towns.' Edith Ennen's work is corroborated by a statement from The IK Workshop Society at www.ikfoundation.org:

The high Middle Ages saw continued use of established techniques for silk manufacture without any changes to speak of, neither in materials nor in tools used. Between the tenth and twelfth centuries, small changes began to appear, though the changes of the thirteenth century were much larger and more radical. In a short time, new fabrics began to appear; hemp and cotton each also had their own particular techniques of manufacture. Known since Roman times, silk remained a rare and expensive material. Byzantine silk farms in Greece and Syria (sixth to eighth centuries), the ones in Calabria and those of the Arabs in Sicily and Spain (eighth to tenth centuries) were able to supply the luxury material in a much greater abundance.

It wasn't that industrial technology was unknown. At this point, textile technology may have been foremost because of the place occupied by public demand and trade in textiles, and silk of course would have been at the forefront of this drive. The Chinese had already been using various mechanical means for some time:

> Chinese sources claim the existence of a machine to unwind silkworm cocoons in AD 1090. The cocoons were placed in a large basin of hot water, the silk would leave the cauldron by tiny guiding rings, and would be wound on to a large spool, thanks to a backward and forward motion. ... The spinning wheel was known by the beginning of the Christian era. The first accepted image of a spinning wheel appears in 1210. There is an image of a silk-spinning machine powered by a waterwheel that dates to 1313. ... More information is known about the looms used. The *Nung Sang Chi Yao*, or *Fundamentals of Agriculture and Sericulture*, compiled around 1210, is rich with pictures and descriptions, many pertaining to silk ... it claims the Chinese looms to be far superior ... it speaks of two types of loom that leave the worker's arms free: the draw loom, which is of Eurasian origin, and the pedal loom which is attributed to East Asian origins. There are many diagrams that originate in the twelfth and thirteenth centuries.
>
> (Source): The IK Workshop Society at
> www.ikfoundation.org

The Crusades were a series of religious wars initiated by the Roman religious authorities aimed at placing the Holy Land back under the rule of Christianity. The Crusades is a loose term, and they did not all happen together. In fact, there were four main Crusades, with fairly long gaps of around forty years between the first three, and it was this third and longest lasting Crusade (1184–1192) in which King Richard I, known as Coeur de Lion, Heart of the Lion, and the elder brother of 'bad King John', took part, and this period which gave rise to the legend of Robin Hood.

1st Crusade 1095–1099
2nd Crusade 1147–1149
3rd Crusade 1184–1192
4th Crusade 1202–1204

The Third Crusade was also the most wide-ranging Crusade and so it is likely that it was the Crusaders of the late twelfth century who were responsible (although perhaps not always legally) for bringing silk to western Europe, initially to the Italian city states. All the Crusaders were, of course, sworn to uphold Christianity and its ideals. The Vatican in Rome was the earthly centre of Roman Catholicism, and the Pope was its head, so it was in Italy that the western European silk industry first began to grow substantially, although it quickly spread to France, one of the other major Catholic countries of western Europe. Subsequently, for political reasons, the papacy moved from Rome to Avignon during the years 1309–1378, becoming known as the Avignon Papacy. There was a great deal of controversy when the papacy returned to Rome and consequently, from 1378–1409, there were two popes, one based in Avignon and one based in Rome, which caused even more problems and confusion. However, during this period, the silk industry flourished in both countries. Guilds were set up to safeguard workers, wages and working practices, subsequently becoming very powerful organisations. Italy at that time was the foremost and richest economy in western Europe, and the main silk centres were in the northern Italian regions of Como, Genoa, Bologna, Venice, Lucca and Florence. During the twelfth century, an Italian Renaissance had begun which was to be the last of the medieval renaissances. It was an exciting and creative time, as interest in the arts and sciences of classical antiquity were revived and flourished. In 1260, two brothers from Venice, Nicolo and

Maffeo Polo, father and uncle of Marco Polo, set out for the Crimea on a trading venture where they met the envoys of Kublai Khan (immortalised by Samuel Coleridge), the grandson of Ghengis Khan. The envoys persuaded the Polo brothers that they should travel on to Cathay (the medieval European name for China) which resulted in marked cultural exchanges between Italy and China. The brothers returned to Venice in 1269 but set out again for Cathay and a return visit to Kublai Khan in 1271, this time with Nicolo's 17-year-old son, Marco. It was Marco Polo who wrote *Silk Road*, a journal of their travels to and from Cathay, a fascinating and unrivalled account of travelling through different lands and cultures from Italy to the Crimea, through western Armenia, across Persia, northern Tibet and inner Mongolia, following the old Silk Road for much of the way, to Kublai Khan's court at Shangtu near modern Beijing. They arrived at Kublai Khan's court in 1275 and spent seventeen years working in his service before eventually returning for home with a small fortune; first sailing to Persia and arriving in 1294, then, for their safety, crossing Persia with an armed escort before making their way back to Venice and arriving there around 1295.

The Byzantine Empire had intended to develop a silk industry using techniques learned from the Persians, who controlled the silk trade along the Silk Road to Byzantium and Europe at that time. However, Byzantium had also managed to continue importing silk from other major urban centres on the Mediterranean. Byzantine techniques paid great attention to the decorative aspects, the weaving techniques for which were taken from Egypt where semple looms, which controlled patterns to be woven, had been used since the fifth century. It was the Arabs, empire-building with their European conquests, who spread sericulture across the Mediterranean, leading to sericulture development in North Africa, Andalucia, Sicily and also Calabria in southern Italy. It is believed that mulberry trees for the silkworms were introduced to southern Italy by Byzantines in the ninth century and that by 1050 Calabria had 24,000 mulberry trees. Catanzaro, in Calabria, which became renowned for its lace, became the first Italian city to introduce silk production sometime between the ninth and eleventh centuries, and sold its wares of silks, velvets and brocades to merchants from Venice, Florence, Lucca and Genoa, as well as those from places further afield such as Spain and Holland. The Crusades also encouraged the techniques of silk production to spread right across western Europe.

Chapter 2

Italian Industrial History before the Black Death 1347–1349

Italy had enjoyed a high degree of civilisation during the days of the Roman Empire and also had the ability, although not necessarily the incentive, to develop technological innovations. For example, the Romans were well aware of water power engineered by water mills, and they actually built a few water mills, but these mills were not really considered necessary since the numbers of slaves and poor people obviated the need for power generated this way; it was felt preferable to employ people power, or, sometimes, animal power supervised by people power. As the complex and enigmatic Roman emperor, Vespasian (AD 9–79), put it, 'Suffer me to find maintenance for the poor people.' Recounting this episode, the historian Suetonius (*c.* AD 69–122) stated that 'Someone offering to convey some immense columns into the Capitol at a small expense by a mechanical contrivance, he [Vespasian] rewarded him very handsomely for his invention, but would not accept his service.' Suetonius believed that these columns were 'probably the colossal statue of Nero afterwards placed in Vespasian's amphitheatre, which derived its name from it.'

This view of providing work for slaves and poor people had been echoed by Augustus (63 BC–AD 14), according to Suetonius, when he rebuilt the city of Rome saying 'he had found a city of bricks but left it of marble.' although Dio (*c.* AD 150–235) records Augustus's words as 'that Rome, which I found built of mud, I shall leave you firm as a rock'.

9

Initiating programmes of building work to provide employment has long been practised and was also carried out in the twentieth century after both world wars. However, in Antiquity and during the first millennium AD in Europe, there were sufficient people to carry out all the types of work required manually. Provision of goods and services had remained at cottage-industry level and there was little need for technological advances or mechanisation.

Post-Roman Europe was initially very much based on farming and cottage industries, and it was agrarian innovation which began to lead the way towards technological innovation. Water mills had been in use since the sixth century, after the end of the Roman era, although they were mostly used for grinding corn. In the seventh century, use of the heavy plough, an invention of Slavic origin, spread across northern Europe, and by the eighth century, the three-field system of crop rotation, which increased production, and therefore prosperity, was in operation. During the ninth century the

horseshoe, which had been known since Celtic times, came into common use which increased the efficient use of horsepower. Horses were stronger and faster and more adaptable than the oxen which had previously been used and this led to increased interest in breeds and importation of the animals from Eastern countries. These agricultural innovations also led to co-operation and team working among the peasants and farmers since, obviously, not everyone could afford a horse or a plough and increased yields would require extra help at harvest times. This in turn led to local communities developing robust systems of self-regulation and self-government to minimise any potential problems. The tenth century marked something of a turning point in western Europe. The water mills, formerly used just for grinding corn, now began to be used for other production purposes.

In China, for instance, they were used for blowing bellows during metal working processes and as a source of power. Now western Europe began to catch up with Chinese technological ideas. More powerful water mills were built whose 'hydraulic energy' could be harnessed in a variety of ways. For example, in Picardy, water mills were adapted with vertical hammers to pound malt in preparation for beer-making. In Normandy, Sweden and Moravia, mills powered sawing of wood, and facilitated paper manufacture at Fabriano, Troyes and Nuremburg. Many were used for fulling cloth in Normandy, France, Germany and England. These extra uses have been described as 'the industrial revolution of the thirteenth century.' Around 1570 a traveller to Bologna described the use of water power in Italy 'to turn various machines to grind grain, to make copper pots and weapons of war, to pound herbs … for dyeing, to spin silk, polish arms, sharpen various instruments, saw planks'.

(The Expansion of Technology 500–1500.
White, Lynn. Fontana, 1972)

As well as watermills there were windmills. It is thought wind power was first harnessed this way in Persia sometime in the sixth or seventh century. Windmills are said to have been brought to Europe by the Crusaders of the twelfth century. The first examples seem to have appeared in Normandy which would be in keeping with this tradition of introducing the use of wind power. It was called 'the winged mill' in a Tudor period description: 'The winged mill which now wants to be driven by the winds is said to have been unknown to the Romans.' (Johannes Stradanus 1523–1605) There were two basic types: 'Those set to operate by the prevailing winds and those that are pivoted to face into chance winds.' (Carlo M. Cipolla. 1976). Originally, the entire mill had to be turned to face the wind until the development of the tower mill in the 1300s where only the top was needed to turn the sails into the wind. Tower mills could generate power equivalent to thirty horses but windmills were subject to an element of nature which could not be controlled. There might be little or no wind for days in European settings, so watermills tended to be more common.

It has been neatly summarised, and this was probably quite a realistic assessment, that

> European technical advancements from the 12th to 14th centuries were either built on long-established techniques in medieval Europe, originating from Roman and Byzantine antecedents, or adapted from cross-cultural exchanges through trading networks with the Islamic world, China, and India. Often, the revolutionary aspect lay not in the act of invention itself, but in its technological refinement and application to political and economic power.
>
> (Source): The IK Workshop Society at
> www.ikfoundation.org

After the Crusades ended with the sacking of Constantinople (now Istanbul) in 1204, the city's silk industry declined and many skilled silk workers left. Some went to France, but 2,000 of them settled in Italy. Lucca's silk industry grew as a result and was further increased by immigrant refugees. This resulted in Chinese silk exports declining while those of Lucca, Genoa, Florence and Venice increased dramatically. 'By the thirteenth century the technology of silk throwing had been mastered in Tuscany. The silk works used water power to run the complex machinery needed ... these were the first mechanised textile mills.' (Mokyr, 1990).

Silk production centred, mainly due to Jewish, Sicilian and Greek immigrants during the twelfth century, in the walled city of

Lucca, its maze of narrow medieval streets filled with craftsmen's houses, and they guarded their monopoly jealously from the twelfth to the fourteenth centuries. However, violent political conflict in the fourteenth century had resulted in many skilled crafts workers fleeing the city of Lucca to Genoa, Florence, Bologna and Venice. Lucca in the twelfth and thirteenth centuries had 'made notable improvements in the technology of silk-throwing devices and promoted the sericulture in the immediate countryside', and it now became 'an economic model for silk production'. Silk production was controlled by merchant entrepreneurs who 'supplied silk fibres to small independent and specialised workshops', for which skilled labour was essential. Lucca's economic development was further enhanced by the growing demand for luxury textiles in western Europe during the Middle Ages.

In the commercial registers of 1371, there were eighty-nine such firms recorded and about 3,000 looms were in use. (*Renaissance Silk for Lucca*. Donald and Monique King. Stockholm. 1988).

In Italy, the story of the silk industry had really begun in Tuscany during the Crusades when some of the Crusaders had brought silk production to western Europe in general, but to France and Italy in particular. Although silk had been a uniquely Chinese industry since Neolithic times, it had spread to Japan by about AD300; and by the middle of the sixth century Byzantines in Greece and Syria, as well as Arabs in Spain and Sicily, had begun silkworm cultivation and silk manufacture. French fashion dictated lighter and less expensive silk production in France, but Italy retained a reputation for luxury silks in brilliant colours. By the beginning of the thirteenth century, demand was such that the technology of the time was beginning to undergo a wide-ranging and important series of changes, but the cataclysm for real change came in the first half of the fourteenth century. It was a time of climatic change, erratic weather and failed harvests culminating in the Great Famine of 1315–1322 when up to 15 per cent of the population of Europe died. Wages fell as the price of grain soared. The European population was weakened by the famine and had not fully recovered when a plague of the Black Death (bubonic plague), which became the worst recorded pandemic in history to date, swept across Europe in 1347–1349, killing up to 60 per cent of the population.

Northern Italy, the developed urban part of the country, was the first place in western Europe to be affected by the Black Death. It had arrived in Genoa on a ship from the Crimean port of Kaffa, which had been infected by members of the Mongol Golden Horde army. It rapidly spread to Bologna, Venice, Pisa, and Florence, which were all part of the main silk industry areas of medieval Italy. Those who could, fled, and those left behind were simply abandoned without help or hope. Boccaccio in *The Decameron* described the symptoms and effects of the Black Death, which was a rapid and efficient killer, as well as the sheer terror which gripped those in areas affected by the plague. Boccaccio wrote:

> Such was the multitude of corpses brought to the churches every day and almost every hour that there was not enough consecrated ground to give them burial, especially since they wanted to bury each person in the family grave, according to the old custom. Although the cemeteries were full, they were forced to dig huge trenches, where they buried the bodies by hundreds. Here they stowed them away like bales in the hold of a ship and covered them with a little earth, until the whole trench was full.

Then, as now, it was financially and socially disadvantaged people who bore the brunt of the suffering. The wealthy could escape – and mostly did in terms of famine and plague – around 70 per cent survived as against 30–40 per cent of poor people.

The plight of the lower and most of the middle classes was even more pitiful to behold. Most of them remained in their houses, either through poverty or in hopes of safety, and fell sick by thousands. Since they received no care and attention, almost all of them died. Many ended their lives in the streets both at night and during the day; and many others who died in their houses were only known to be dead because the neighbours smelled their decaying bodies. Dead bodies filled every corner.

(*The Decameron*. Boccaccio, Giovanni. 1349).

The people of Florence and Venice eventually managed to quell their panic for long enough to think of rational methods of protection against the plague. These two city states pioneered the ideas of quarantine and lockdown, promoting face coverings and 'keeping your distance'. Mass burials were common, carried out by beggars, their faces shrouded in rags.

However, once the pandemic was over, there was a high price to pay, even for the rich, because now there were very few left to do the work and in the case of some villages, there was no one left at all. The lucrative silk industry suffered particularly badly and when the plague had gone those who had survived discovered they could not revive the industry by themselves. There were simply insufficient working people left to cope and carry out the various tasks of producing the beautiful silks and velvets or the strong silken yarn of organzine. The Italians realised that, if they were to revive their silk industry, they needed help but there was no human help available. Necessity being the mother of invention, invention is exactly what happened.

Chapter 3

Italian Silk-Spinning and Throwing Machinery Powered by Wind and Water in Medieval Times

At the start of the thirteenth century, a primitive form of milling the silk threads was already in use. In 1221, Jean de Garlande's dictionary, and in 1226, Étienne Boileau's *Livre des métiers* (Tradesman's Handbook) enumerated many types of devices which were almost certainly doubling machines. The instruments used were further perfected in Bologna between 1270 and 1280. From the start of the fourteenth century, many documents allude to the use of 'devices that were quite complex'. (Source): The IK Workshop Society at www.ikfoundation.org

A basic definition of throwing is given in simple detail in *Silk, its Production and Manufacture* Hooper, Luther. Pitman. 1919).

> Throwing (sometimes called Spinning). The next process is sometimes called spinning, but more properly throwing. Spinning implies not only twisting the thread, but joining, by means of twisting, numbers of short filaments together into a continuous thread. Throwing, however, merely means the closer and regulated twisting of an already loosely made, compound, continuous thread. The throwing frame is fitted up with a great number of spindles to which one person can attend. The work is, however, very responsible and requires great accuracy so that a competent mechanic

has to be in charge. ... The effective action of the throwing frame depends upon the revolving of two sets of bobbins at different, nicely adjusted speeds. By the proportions of the two revolutions, one to the other, more, or less, amount of twist is given to the thread thrown. Threads are required to have various amounts of twist on them, according to the purpose for which they are intended.

The initial process in the production of silk yarn was reeling, the unwinding of the silk filaments from the cocoons of the silkworms. The cocoons were soaked in boiling water which softened the sticky binding of the filaments but killed the metamorphosing caterpillars within the cocoon. Rods, to which the filaments of silk would adhere, were dipped in hot water and the filaments then wound on reels. Individual filaments are too delicate to be reeled on their own and they become thinner towards the centre of the cocoon, so between three and eight filaments are usually reeled together. The method of carrying out this process in sixteenth-century Florence was similar to that used in thirteenth-century China. After reeling, the threads from the hanks of silk yarn were cleaned, two or three threads twisted together by a spindle wheel to give additional strength, and the yarn was then wound on to spools or bobbins by a spool winder. This process is known as silk throwing and produces the twisted silk thread known as organzine. The organzine is then often twisted again with more threads, in a process known as doubling which gives it greater strength. In silk manufacture, reeling and twisting replace 'proper' spinning.

It is a reversal of the spinning process applied to wool, linen and cotton, and it is made possible by the continuity of the silk filament. Whereas the spinning process was intermittent with a spindle wheel [which twisted the silk filaments] the twisting of silk is continuous.

(*A History of Technology.* Singer, Charles E. and others. Oxford Clarendon Press. 1956)

During the thirteenth century, there were a number of technical improvements in 'the reeling and throwing of silk in Italy' and quite sophisticated twisting mills were invented in the late thirteenth century. There is very little record of these machines because the Italians guarded their silk secrets jealously, but a fourteenth-century document from Lucca and a drawing from a Florentine manuscript of 1487 show that the earliest example of a twisting mill is remarkably similar to the detailed illustration of a water-powered silk mill by Vittorio di Zonca in 1607. In the middle of the fourteenth century, crucially around the time of the devastation caused by the 1347–1349 pandemic of the Black Death, Bolognino di Borghesano, a merchant from Lucca, was granted a licence to build a hydraulic silk mill in Bologna. According to Charles Singer, a document from Lucca stated that:

the mill had two rows of twelve reels with ten spindles to each reel, one thousand spools, two hundred and forty spindles and a similar number of caps and glass sockets for the spindles ... in 1385 a mill is described having four rows of spindles and reels, another had five rows of sixteen reels and six spindles per reel. Each row [therefore] had ninety-six spindles and the mill a total of four hundred and eighty spindles The caps were of different weights: light ones for thin yarns and heavier ones for coarse yarns. A mill of 1331 had two rows of spindles with one hundred and twenty in each row. These twisting mills, driven by

undershot waterwheels, were introduced to Florence
and Venice by workers from Lucca.

(*A History of Technology*. Singer, Charles E. and
others. Oxford Clarendon Press. 1956)

In modern times the word 'mill' has become synonymous with
'factory', but this is a misnomer. It comes from the Latin 'mola'
meaning a grindstone for milling corn. The original building
would be small and intended to house just one process which
would be operated by one person. From the Middle Ages, the use
of the word expanded from just grinding corn to other processes,
especially those used in textile production. Water-powered mills
were in common use by the twelfth century, but by the early
thirteenth century, a 'winged' mill (windmill with sails) had been
brought to Europe, almost certainly by the Crusaders, from the
East where it had been developed in Persia around the seventh
century AD. The idea of exploiting wind energy instead of, or in
addition to, water was new and exciting. However, the 'winged'
mills were primarily used for grinding corn and mills powered
by waterwheels were mainly used in textile manufacturing
processes. There were differing designs of mill, depending upon
the type of use, sporting different names. By the seventeenth
century, the term 'Piedmont silk mill' identified a particular
type of silk-throwing machinery, which was, in fact, the same
as the Bologna Mill, encased in a building, around the same
size as a corn-grinding mill, but worked by water power. The
'miller' would work the machinery with assistance from a small
group of journeymen (derived from the French *journée* meaning
day because they were paid on a daily basis). Each journeyman
would first complete an apprenticeship, and then he could, if he
wished, go on to become a master, but most continued to work as
employees. It was small-scale teamwork rather than the modern
idea of a large factory.

There appear to have been two basic types of silk-throwing mills: The Bolognese mill which originated in Bologna and was the result of Borghesano's work; and the Milanese mill which originated in Milan (Comino and Gasparetti 2020). There were three main differences between the two types of mill. (*La Seta in Italia*. Poni, Carlo, 2009)

The Bolognese mill

- was hydraulically powered
- had spools not reels
- had mechanical winders to perform the spooling

The Milanese mill

- was hand powered
- had reels not spools
- the reeling operation was carried out manually

There was also mention of a Genoa silk mill but this is believed to have been simply an adaptation of the Bolognese mill. There is no mention of a specific Piedmont silk mill, but that is not to say there wasn't one. It could simply have been a further refined adaptation of the Bolognese mill. The images of a silk-throwing machine in di Zonca's book and in the Prato museum are of a Bolognese silk mill, and it was the plans of this superior hydraulically powered silk-throwing mill which John Lombe copied and brought back from Italy. The workings of the Bolognese silk mill had been improved by the generations of engineers who followed Borghesano. Rollers had been added as evidenced by sixteenth-century sources and the detailed plans drawn by di Zonca at the end of the sixteenth century. He had drawn his plan of the Bologna silk-throwing machine and labelled it as a Piedmont silk mill. Possibly, he could have drawn the machine in Piedmont whose silk industry had thrived during the sixteenth century but had steadily declined during the seventeenth century. However, there is no doubt that it was a Bolognese silk mill.

Borghesano's large mill is the first known example of an early silk manufactory, or factory, as opposed to a small individual silk mill. It was the model for the future factories of the Industrial Revolution. So, Bolognino di Borghesano, a fourteenth-century Italian silk merchant from Lucca, and not Richard Arkwright, an eighteenth-century English entrepreneur, was the real 'father of the factory system'. Four hundred years later, Arkwright simply copied and exploited an earlier 'factory system', which had already been copied by John Lombe in Derby. The word 'mill', signifies both a small building, worked by wind sails or a waterwheel and supervised by one or two workers, for grinding corn into flour or crushing fruit for cider, and a very large building with hundreds of workers and dozens of machines for the manufacture of textiles, initially using hydraulic power, then steam power, followed, from the nineteenth century onwards, by gas or electric power. Early Italian silk mills were not like the mills of the Industrial Revolution, but were about the size of a large wind/water mill building, needing only two or three people to operate them to join broken threads or replace spools and reels. The silk yarn was then wound in hanks by a simple rotary wheel such as that shown in an *Ypres Book of Trades* (1310). Previously all the work would have been done by human hands, but industrial mechanisation was designed to cope with the lack of manpower after the Great Famine and the pandemic of the Black Death.

The millennial span of the Middle Ages has the interest of being the period during which Europe built up the self-confidence and the technical competence which, after 1500, enabled it to invade the rest of the world, conquering, looting, trading and colonising.

> (*The Expansion of Technology 500–1500*.
> White, Lynn. Fontana, 1972)

The effects of the Black Death pandemic of 1347–1349 on labour, production, trade and the economy in all areas, was marked. Before the pandemic, the population of Florence had been around 100,000. Thirty years later, in 1378, the population had fallen to 55,000 and by 1427 was only 37,000. Silk workers could command higher wages although there were simply not enough highly skilled workers. Silk production costs had increased as well due to the rising price of silk and special dyes, and it had been decided to target the high end of the market to justify the rise in wage costs for the silk workers. This, in turn, required people with good sales and marketing skills and experience in sourcing raw materials, but it also raised the question of how to keep pace with demand. Florence had become a major silk producer by the fifteenth century, although this was based mainly on silk workers from Lucca who had emigrated to Florence as refugees from political strife in 1314. Their arrival had coincided with an increase in demand for luxury silk fabrics which formed the basis for the establishment of a silk production industry in Florence 'as the story of *The Guild of Por Santa Maria* (the guild representing the silk workers and producers) shows, it took a century before the silk industry became a major force in Florence.' However,

> by the middle of the fifteenth century the silk industry had an important phase of expansion; total production figures for silk for the period 1430–47 show a fourfold increase. Florence produced the most luxurious kinds of

fabrics, including lampas, figured velvets, and brocades enhanced with gold and silver threads and elaborate embroidery.

> (*The Economy of Renaissance Florence.*
> Goldthwaite, Richard A. JHU Press. 2009)

After the fourteenth-century Black Death pandemic, the powerful guilds had been forced to relax certain of their strict regulations for the textile industries, mostly involving quality of materials and certain processes, on account of the loss of people power, and in the silk industry the use of water-powered mills was increasing. There were other developments too, of course:

> In the second half of the fifteenth century, draw-loom technology was first brought to France by an Italian weaver from Calabria, known as Jean le Calabrais, who was invited to Lyon by Louis XI. He introduced a new kind of machine which was able to work the yarns faster and more precisely. Over the years, improvements to the loom were ongoing.
>
> (Source): The IK Workshop Society at
> www.ikfoundation.org

By 1472, there were 84 workshops and over 7,000 craftsmen in Florence, and in 1519 Catanzaro established 'a consulate of the silk craft, charged with regulating and checking the various stages of a production.' At this point, the city had over 500 looms; and by 1660, its silk industry kept 1,000 looms busy, employing at least 5,000 people, and selling silk textiles to England, France Spain and Venice.

Florence was also a centre of banking and commerce, so the textile industry grew rapidly to meet the demands of the European markets for whom silken clothing was a status symbol.

'Dress was employed as a primary visual means by medieval and Renaissance elite to manifest rank and magnificence publicly.' (William J. Connell). The French were fond of wearing silk for similar reasons, and Lyon became a major centre of silk production along with towns, such as Carcassonne, in Provence. However, even the French could not match the Italian manufacture of organzine, and, consequently, were dependent upon Italian exports. England suffered from the same problems, although its silk industry was much inferior to that of the French.

Silk machinery, such as reeling machines and flyers for twisting and doubling, had been used in China since around 100BC and had arrived in Europe during the thirteenth century via the Crusaders. However, draw looms used for weaving silk had been known in Europe since post-Roman times. Water power for these machines was introduced in both China and Europe in around the same period of the thirteenth and fourteenth centuries. Each generation of workers and engineers modified and improved the mechanical designs and workings of these machines, adding refinements and increasing efficiency. Many of these exciting mechanical innovations of the Continent were not really adopted in England until the eighteenth century. This may have been because the major English textile was wool until this time, followed by linen. Silk was more a cottage industry worked by hand. Processes of cotton manufacture in England did not really begin until the early 1770s.

Weaving is defined in *A History of Technology* as 'the interlacing of one series of filaments or threads, known as the warp, with another series of filament or threads, known as the weft.'

Warp threads (down) are longitudinal and weft threads (across) are transverse or latitudinal. Simple looms were known in the Neolithic period and in Antiquity and the draw loom was popular. However, by the thirteenth century the most widely used loom in Europe was the horizontal frame loom and the *Ypres Book of Trades* (1310) is a little mine of information together with helpful sketches of weaving machinery. The *Encyclopaedia Britannica* states that 'in the Shang (or Yin) period (eighteenth to twentieth centuries BC) in China some bronzes show traces of a twill damask pattern suggesting that they were produced on a horizontal frame loom with treadles', but the thirteenth-century European horizontal loom, as portrayed in the *Book of Trades* was a far more sophisticated version:

> It had a stout box-like framework stretching the warp horizontally between a warp-beam at the back and breast-beam in front … and also permits the introduction of a shedding-mechanism to lift and lower alternate warp threads by treadles … with two or more heddles (a component usually made of cord through the eye of which a strand of warp is threaded to keep it flat and taut) and the shuttle (the tool around which the weft is wound to pass it through the warp threads) is passed through.
>
> (*A History of Technology*. Singer, Charles E. and others. Oxford Clarendon Press. 1956, and *Encyclopaedia Britannica*)

After weaving, the cloth undergoes the final processes of fulling (cleaning and shrinking of material so that fibres adhere to each other) and finishing (cropping, bleaching, dyeing and pressing). Although silk was woven and finished like other textiles, it was in the initial processes of reeling and twisting the silk (known as throwing) where the English could not match the Italian quality, quantity and speed of turnout for organzine thread; it was this which eventually led to John Lombe's act of industrial espionage in the early eighteenth century.

Chapter 4

Italian Medieval and Renaissance Engineers and Inventors

The Renaissance, which marked the transition from medieval to modernity in western Europe, really began in Florence during the fourteenth century and marked great social changes. It quickly spread to Venice, which had created its own empire based on participation in the Crusades (1096–1204), and on the travels between 1271 and 1295 of one of Venice's most famous sons, Marco Polo (1254–1324), along the Silk Road to China (where he served under Kublai Khan) and his wider travels as he returned from China. Although there are several proposed dates for this rediscovery of classical history and achievements, this new flowering of ideas and literature, arts and sciences, this rebirth of culture, the most commonly accepted dates are from around 1350 to 1620, but 'from the twelfth to the fifteenth century the Italians were in the forefront not only of economic development but also of technological progress.' (Carlo Cipolla 1976). The Italians certainly led the field in art, architecture, science and invention before and during the period that Cipolla states after which 'this primacy passed to the Dutch and the English,' with, of course, a little help from the Italians. However, the foundations of the mechanical engineering, which led to the development of the textile industry during the eighteenth and nineteenth-century Industrial Revolution in England, were laid in Italy during the thirteenth century. In addition to the numbers of well-known artists, architects, scientists and writers, this medieval Italian Renaissance also produced an unusual and important group of polymath artists and engineers: Mariano di Jacopo, known as Taccola, (1382–1453); Francesco di Giorgio Martini (1459–1501); Leonardo da Vinci (1452–1519); Vittorio di Zonca (1568–1603); Galileo Galilei (1564–1642). It was an exciting age of exploration, invention, and adventure, in which it was considered normal and acceptable practice for those who came after to improve upon the works of those who had gone before.

Mariano di Jacopo (known as Taccola)

Considered to be the earliest of this polymath group, Jacopo was born in Siena in 1352, although he was commonly known as Taccola, (Italian for jackdaw) and nicknamed the Sienese Archimedes. His 'day jobs' appear to have been in administrative posts (notary, secretary, supervisory) but he is chiefly remembered for his two manuscripts: *De Ingeneis* (Of Engines), written as four books which took thirty years (1419–49) to complete, and *De Machinis* (Of Machines). The State Library of Florence holds the originals, which were written in Italian – with a touch of medieval manuscript design and flourish – but the British Library holds a manuscript (Add MSS 34113) described as 'containing a compilation of treatises on natural philosophy and mechanics along with numerous mechanical designs, principally selections from the works *De Ingeneis* (1433) and *De Machinis* (1449) by the Sienese engineer Mariano Taccola (c1382–1458), and the Codicetto (?1460s–70s) by the Sienese architect Francesco di Giorgio Martini.'

The British Library description of Taccola's work includes:

> numerous mechanical designs in outline drawing, usually tinted with brown, pink and green washes, including apparatus for scientific experiments, hydraulic systems, devices for moving heavy loads, mills, fortresses,

siege machines, weapons, devices for crossing water, carpentry joints, devices for catching fish, devices for operating bellows, chimneys, a sheepfold, battering rams, ladders, ships, fountains, a centaur costume, diving suits, parachutes, cannons, clocks, surveying techniques, systems for raising columns.

His drawings were neat and detailed, although sometimes lacking in the correct perspective, despite Taccola being a colleague of Filippo Brunelleschi, 'the father of linear perspective', but he drew 'the lifting devices and reversible gear systems which Brunelleschi devised for the construction of the dome of Florence cathedral'. The Duomo, as the cathedral is known today, still dominates the city of Florence.

Francesco di Giorgio Martini

Born in Siena in 1439, Martini was an Italian architect, engineer, painter (of the Sienese School), sculptor, and writer; he was also considered 'a visionary architectural theorist'. The *Bibiloteca Apostolica Vaticana*, Vatican City, holds *Ms.Lat.Urbinas* 1757 (BAV) which is a miniature codex of 191 leaves, that includes both Taccola's work and studies by Martini, involving mills (floating mills with horizontal and vertical wheels, mills powered by treadmills), bucket pumps, pile drivers, winches, cranes, carts, and haulage machines for lifting and displacing weights. There is little doubt that he was influenced by Taccola, but his natural mechanical creativity embraced a number of different disciplines such as war devices (including siege ladders, boat sinking devices, hooks for scaling walls, exploding projectiles, fire bellows) as well as 'self-moving ploughs' and a paddle-boat operated by a treadwheel. He improved Siena's aqueduct and fountain system to increase the city's water supply while his experience as a war engineer was as valued as his architectural innovations. He wrote *Trattado di Architectura* (A Treatise on Architecture) in 1475 but it was never published.

Vittorio di Zonca

Born in Padua in 1568, Vittorio di Zonca was not destined for a long life. He died in 1603 aged just 35. Little is known about him except that he was an engineer and a writer, and his major contribution to history was to write *Novo Teatro di Machine et Edificii* literally translated as *New Theatre of Machines and Buildings*. It is a very practical book, illustrated with clear and detailed drawings, many based on Martini's work. The book includes a section on textile machinery, one of which, a machine labelled 'a Piedmont Silk Mill', is actually a copy of the Bologna silk mill. This provided the basic blueprint for the water frame that revolutionised textile production in England nearly 200 years later. Zonca is a strong advocate of water power. On the page opposite his diagram of the Bolognese silk-throwing model, *Filatoio ad acqua*, literally 'spinning from water', he writes enthusiastically, almost bubbling over, that

> *Bellissima anzi marauigliosa è la fabrica del Filatoio ad acqua, pericoche si vede is essa tanti mouimenti di ruote, fusi, totelle, & altre forti di legni per trauerso, perlo lungo, & per diagonal; che l'occhio vi si smarisce dentro à pensarui; come l'ingegno humano habbia potuto capire tanta varieta di cose, di tanti mouimenti contranj mossi da vna sol ruota, che hà il moto inannimato. Quali Filatori non pur filano la seta, cioe l'auolgon attornon i naspi, ma la intorceno piu, e meno,*

secondo il bisogno, si per lauorarla, com per tesserne i panni di seta, Primieramente ha questa Machina il motore gagliardo, che è l'acqua corrente, la quale si rinchiude in vn canale, con la sue porta, & l'argano per a prirla; si come è costume de fare ne i Molini terragni, & dar il mouimento alla ruota. Questa quanto sara Maggiore, tanto farà, più al proposito, ma non però tanto che le pale, ouer pinné, delequali è circondata la ruota, si come nelle altre, non pelchino almeno quattro di esse nell'acqua.

His enthusiasm translates clearly and poetically across the centuries:

Beautiful, or better still, marvellous indeed is the water-powered textile mill, for one can see in it so many wheel movements, spools, totella [smaller wheels?] and other remarkable examples of wooden structures positioned diagonally, length wise and horizontally; so that the eye becomes lost just by thinking about it and how human ingenuity could have possibly devised such a variety of convoluted movements that are caused by such an inanimate object as a wheel. The spinners not only work the silk but also wrap it around the spools, tightly or loosely as required, in order to prepare it to become silk clothes. This machine is primarily driven by such a vigorous engine as running water itself, which is channelled via an inlet and then directed to force a wheel as is customary for all windmills. The bigger the force, the better the outcome, as long as at least four of its shovels at a time manage to hit the water.

(translated by Simona Continente. 2021)

However, the plans drawn by di Zonca were not of his own inventions, but of engineers who had gone before him, including Borghesano, Leonardo da Vinci, Martini and Taccola. The book was not published until 1607, four years after di Zonca's death. It was republished in 1624, and in 1627 a gentleman named Joseph Schreck translated the captions of the plates into Chinese for a Chinese publication, *Diagrams and Explanations of the Wonderful Machines of the far West*. Over 200 years later, John Lombe would pay with his life for going to Italy to copy plans of Italian silk throwing and spinning machinery, but these same plans were contained in di Zonca's book, a copy of which has been on the shelves of the Bodleian Library in Oxford since 1656.

Galileo Galilei

Galilei was born in Pisa in 1564 and moved to Florence when he was 10. He was an astronomer, physicist, engineer and writer variously described as 'the father of astronomy', 'the father of modern physics', 'the father of the scientific method' and 'the father of modern science', and he was often a controversial figure. He is mostly known for his support of Copernicus's theory of the daily rotation of the Earth and its revolving around the sun, which was at odds with the Church's views in his day. He also observed the phases of Venus, the satellites of Jupiter and the rings of Saturn. He pioneered the telescope, invented a thermoscope (the forerunner of the thermometer), and did essential work on the theory of swinging pendulums that resulted in the development of accurate timepieces. Galileo was inspired by Florence and the Renaissance artists, although he taught mathematics at the University of Pisa and, subsequently, geometry, mechanics and astronomy at the University of Padua, one of the oldest universities in the world, established in 1222. Although his knowledge in the field of mechanics was sophisticated, he made fewer engineering contributions than the others in this unique group of polymaths to any industrial revolution in textile production because his real passion was for astronomy.

Leonardo da Vinci

During the summer of 1451 among the cornfields of Tuscany, bright with ripening wheat and brilliant red poppies, a love affair between a 'low born' farmer's daughter from Anchiano, named Caterina, and Ser Piero, the Vinci notary's son, produced one of the greatest minds the world has ever known: Leonardo da Vinci. Catarina (di Meo Lippi or Buti del Vacca – her surname is uncertain), classed as simply a peasant girl, was far below Ser Piero Fruosino di Antonio da Vinci, to give him his full title, in the social hierarchy, so Catarina and Piero were quickly married to other people. However, their affair may have been a genuine love story because, unusually for the fifteenth century, both parents were closely involved in the upbringing of their son. Leonardo spent his infancy and early childhood with his mother. When he was 5 or 6, he moved from his mother's home in Anchiano to live with his father in Vinci, a village a couple of kilometres away, so that his father could oversee his education and his apprenticeship. Leonardo's stepmother had no children of her own and grew to love Leonardo like a son. When he was 14, he was apprenticed to Andrea del Verrocchio, a renowned Italian painter who lived and worked in Florence. Leonardo has been termed 'a universal genius', a man of 'unquenchable curiosity and feverishly inventive imagination'. He was a talented artist known for his stunning and beautiful paintings such as *The Last Supper* and the *Mona Lisa*, but he also left behind a collection of notebooks filled with designs and inventions for a wide variety of technology and machinery, including aeroplanes, helicopters, parachutes, tanks, submarines, a double hull for ships, and an 'adding machine'. Leonardo owned a copy of Martini's work and was undoubtedly influenced by him in certain respects, but he had a much broader portfolio. His discoveries and drawings embraced the fields of anatomy, civil engineering, geology, optics and hydro dynamics, although, like Martini, he never published his findings. That task fell to posterity. Among his work was a 'winged spindle designed to perform the stretching, twisting and winding operations simultaneously on three consecutive stretches of thread … the operations were then repeated as the thread fed into the machine … and was the basis for the later development of the continuous spinning machine.' (Museo di Storia della Scienza, Florence).

Leonardo also invented an automated bobbin winder, which was produced during his lifetime, and he left drawings of improvements he made to existing silk-spinning machinery as well. Two hundred and fifty years after his death, his contribution to silk-spinning machinery would become part of a prototype for the water frame. In his book, *A History of Mechanical Inventions* (Rev.ed. 1954), Abbott Payson Usher states that 'the unique distinction of Leonardo as an engineer, however, is most strikingly displayed by the manner in which his work meets the qualifications set down by Reuleaux to mark the beginning of a science of machinery.' This was defined as seeing separate groups of mechanisms or parts of a single whole machine as unique to that particular machine, rather than as parts of a type of machinery. For this reason, every machine would be individually and painstakingly described. Leopold, a writer of 1724, recognised the difference between mechanisms and machines, but it was not until the first Polytechnic School was founded in Paris during 1794 that any real distinction was made between the study of mechanisms and the study of machinery. Leonardo's notebooks confirm that, as both a talented engineer and technician, he clearly recognised this distinction, which marked the beginning of modern mechanical engineering, making sketches of mechanical elements and studies of specific problems connected with some of the machines contemporary with his time. Sigmund Freud wrote of Leonardo that he was 'like a man who awoke too early in the darkness, while the others were still all asleep'. Leonardo saw art and science as complementary, and he began a series of notebooks which fell into four broad categories: painting; architecture; mechanics; anatomy; in which he scribbled his ideas and inventions. He saw and understood so much, but he was not a finisher and his notebooks remained unpublished; so many projects and observations left unfulfilled.

Leonardo's work is arranged within four codexes:

1. Atlanticus (flight, weaponry, music, maths, botany, mechanics, war, astronomy, philosophy)
2. Leicester (Renaissance art, science, thinking, creativity)
3. Arundel (mechanics and geometry)
4. Urbinas (painting; expression, character emotions … painting is a science)

Marco Cianchi wrote a book *Leonardo da Vinci's Machines* (Becocci Editore. 1988 edition). The book includes a new machine involved in textile manufacture. Further information is held by the Leonardian Library of Vinci.

Leonardo would doubtless have improved on existing textile machinery, but this item was his personal contribution to the textile industry. He had already invented two machines for twisting rope strands and then, using similar principles, he invented 'a fin spindle with many more strands arranged in a semi-circle around a drum on which the pulleys wind themselves'. The fin spindle allows the machine to stretch, twist and spool at the same time at three different points of the same thread. The spindle and the fin move simultaneously, but each of them makes a different number of rotations. The fin twists the thread and permits spooling by rotating more rapidly than the spindle. The spindle is also subject to an alternating motion as well as the rotation. It 'comes and goes' allowing the thread to wind in regular spirals over the whole length of the spool. For this operation, Leonardo also designed 'a special machine separately for spinning bobbins'. Leonardo's drawings and diagrams for his machines are neat and precise with explanations written by the side of each one; the unique record of a unique mind.

Chapter 5

Savants in Eighteenth-Century Italy

Although Genoa, Piedmont, Florence, Lucca, Pisa and Venice had been the main areas of the silk industry, by the beginning of the eighteenth century the Genoese and Piedmont silk industries were in decline; Lucca and Pisa had simply become part of the province of Florence. Venice, which had always concentrated on velvets, was more concerned with trade and markets than with production. By the time John Lombe arrived in 1716, Lucca, Prato (Florence), and Bologna were the main silk-producing areas, while Venice concentrated on velvets and merchandising silk. Italian silk and organzine thread remained highly prized, and led the market, but the Italians guarded their silk industry closely.

However, there was a plague of industrial espionage in eighteenth-century Europe. John Lombe was either the first, or one of the first 'spies', and he chose to go about it in a different way from the others. The favourite method was that of 'savants', men of mainly scientific backgrounds who undertook 'intelligent travel'. As Paola Bertucci notes: 'in the course of the eighteenth century, the gathering of information through travel became a common means of rationalising the exploitation of resources, with intelligent travellers becoming increasingly crucial for the political economy of the state.' These travellers denied any idea of espionage, claiming they were just admiring the wonders of industrial progress. The silk industry attracted this attention because the Italians held the secret of efficiently manufacturing strong fine double twisted silk threads for organzine, essential to manufacturing silk goods of quality. There was a celebrated case just twenty years after John

Lombe's successful act of industrial espionage in the silk mills of Florence. His premature death from poisoning shortly afterwards had not seemed to deter others. Perhaps the rewards were too great. The French, Italy's greatest rivals in European silk production, had been desperate to get their hands on Italy's silk production secrets but needed to be careful and circumspect after John Lombe's fate. Paola Bertucci tells the story of how, in 1749, the French Bureau of Commerce decided to commission a study of the silk industry in Piedmont, even though this was in decline at the time. A clever decision perhaps not to focus on the larger more obvious centre of Florence, which was still smarting from the John Lombe episode of 1717 and therefore perhaps more on the alert. Jean-Antoine Nollet, who had 'a background in the mechanical arts', was chosen as the 'savant' for this task. He announced his intention to visit Piedmont as 'a celebrated member of the Academy of Sciences'. However, his best credential was that he 'was already known to the Piedmontese Court because he had been the physics tutor to the Crown Prince in 1738'. Nollet told the Crown Prince that his reason for coming to Italy was 'a philosophical duel' because Italian scientists were claiming the medical benefits of electricity and he wanted to see for himself. The Crown Prince also took him on a tour of an Italian silk manufactory because he considered Nollet's 'learned curiosity was absolutely natural', despite the misgivings of those actually involved in the silk trade. Clearly the lessons learned from the John Lombe affair had already been forgotten in Piedmont.

Chapter 6

The English Silk Industry and the Growth of other English Textile Industries

Wool and flax had been the main textiles both used and manufactured in England since prehistoric times. Flax, a natural crop used for both food and fibres which prefers cooler regions for growth, was hardy enough to be cultivated in many areas, except for those with clay or sandy soils. Its pale blue flowers earned it the name of the 'wee blue blossom' in Ireland. Flax fibres were spun into linen and used mainly for bedding, such as sheets and pillowcases, and later for underwear garments; flax seeds were used to produce linseed oil. The terrain of the country lent itself well to sheep rearing and wool was the most common textile in use from pre-history until the eighteenth century. Wool has been described 'as ancient as the hills and as modern as moonflight'. (Sheep Centre). In medieval times, English wool was much prized on the Continent. East Anglia was a major wool production area. The local breeds of sheep from that region gave fine long-haired wool (which did not require the shrinking process of fulling designed to give a firmer fabric) that was woven into worsted cloth, taking its name from the Norfolk village of Worsted. Silk was not completely unknown in England. One of the earliest references comes from the eighth century. 'Offa, King of Mercia, received a present of two silken vests from the Emperor Charlemagne in 790.' (*The Silk Industry*. Warner, Frank. Dianes, London. 1921). The same writer goes on to say that, although Norman nobles wore silk in the twelfth to fourteenth centuries, their silken apparel was not made in England but obtained from Continental merchants. A statute, issued by Henry III in 1225, states that 'merchant strangers coming into this realm shall be well used … shall have their safe and sure conduct to depart out of England, to come into England … .to buy and sell without any manner of evil tolls.' It was the medieval way of protecting trade with foreign countries.

Edward III (1325–1375) re-iterated a similar statute in 1344: 'The sea shall be open to all manner of merchants to pass with their merchandise when it shall please them.' Edward was instrumental in bringing the first Flemish weavers to England in 1331. Having been impressed by their skills when he was away fighting on the Continent, he encouraged many to come and settle in England, and by doing this he laid the foundations of the textile industry for which England would become renowned. The first reference to silk in the statute books comes in 1363 mentioning 'simple silk weaving' and imports of 'silks, velvets, satins and damasks' from Italy.

A statue of Edward III stands in a niche of Manchester Town Hall in recognition of his contribution to the local textile industry. Connected to this is a romantic story of the Radclyffe family of Ordsall Hall, now in modern-day Salford, a city adjacent to Manchester. Sir John de Radclyffe was instrumental in helping Edward III depose his father, Edward II, in 1325, and then safely conducting Philippa of Hainault to England in the spring of 1326 when she became the wife of Edward III. In 1344, the manor of Ordsall first came into the hands of Sir John de Radclyffe. Unlike many of his contemporaries, who fled abroad during the Black Death of 1347–1349 Sir John had stayed behind, enlarging the town of Salford, helping to cultivate abandoned land, building new houses for the Flemish weavers, encouraging their developing textile industry, and gaining the support of Queen Philippa for his ventures. Today he is widely credited with establishing the textile industry in Lancashire. Ordsall Hall became his home, although he did not survive the later outbreak of the Black Death in 1361–1362.

Nearly 250 years later, the Star Chamber of Ordsall Hall is said to have been where the Gunpowder Plot of 1605 was hatched at a safe distance from London. The Hall still stands, and the Star Chamber has survived, a beautiful tranquil room with a midnight blue ceiling full of stars, a world within a world far removed from the twenty-first century. However, the fields and the sheep have moved on too, and today much of the country's sheep farming is largely confined to mountains, hills and moorlands.

The Black Death pandemic of 1347–1349 was the worst recorded pandemic in history which killed nine out of ten in some English villages. The woollen industry suffered badly and there are several remains of 'ghost villages' where the entire population died. There are also several places where the church is at some distance from the centre of the extant village, indicating a location shift, necessitated by the Black Death, to a site further distant from the graveyard for reasons of hygiene. In 1992, Connie Willis published her novel, *Doomsday Book* a time travel fantasy in which Oxford students from 2054/55 go back in time to study the Middle Ages. One of them is inadvertently trapped in 1348 as the result of an influenza pandemic in their own time. Connie Willis had done her homework on that period of history, and she lays bare the desolation and deprivations caused by the Black Death, recording with a painful poignancy the 'utter devastation of the worst recorded pandemic in history'. The people of that time regarded the pandemic of 1348 as a punishment from God but they had no idea what dreadful crime they could have committed to make God so angry. They did not understand how or why it had spread. They had no vaccines and no defences. People went crazy with fear and panic. Others huddled in their damp drab little huts refusing to see or speak to anyone. Doors of dwellings infected by the plague were marked with a large cross. Whole families died and there was no one left to bury the bodies. The quarantine, or shielding and social distancing to use modern terminology, which finally broke the pandemic of 1347–1349 by starving the Black Death of hosts, had been a Florentine/ Venetian idea, one which the Derbyshire village of Eyam famously copied in 1666, when bales of cloth, infested with rat fleas carrying the Black Death, arrived in the village. The inhabitants sacrificed themselves to prevent the Black Death from spreading over the north of England. By the time the 1666 plague came to an end, those who remained were overwhelmed with shock, grief and depression, but slowly the natural urge to survive, and an awareness that life could and should go on, took over. The death toll had again reduced the population to a point where there was no longer enough labour to do the jobs necessary either for personal survival or national economy, and it was time to consider new ways of doing things.

However, even in 1347–1349, the plague had not killed everyone, and by 1455, 'silk women and spinsters of silk' were given legal protection against imports of unwrought (still in a natural state and not processed) silk followed by further restrictions in 1463 and 1482 on imports of 'small silk goods' which were already being made in England. Samuel Sholl, writing in 1811, summarised the early history of silk manufacture in England:

> There was a company of silk women, in England, so early as the year 1455, but these were probably employed in the needle-works of silk and thread, as we find that various sorts of small haberdashery of silk were manufactured here in 1482 but Italy supplied England, and all other parts, with the broad silk manufacture, til the year 1489. In 1521 the French commenced a silk manufacture.

During the 'golden reign' of Elizabeth I, French and Flemish refugees – the Walloons and Huguenots – many of whom were skilled silk workers, had fled religious persecution and came to England settling mainly in Canterbury and Norwich where they were known as 'The Strangers'. Although the Edict of Nantes in 1598, granting religious tolerance in France, reduced the numbers of refugees considerably, a certain amount of prejudice and mistrust of The Strangers remained in England. King James I, however, recommended the French silk manufacture very highly, wishing to see it introduced into England, and Sholl continues:

> about the year 1620, broad silk manufacture was introduced into this country and prosecuted with great vigour and advantage. In 1629, the silk manufacture became so considerable in London, that the silk throwsters of the city, and parts adjacent, were incorporated under the name of Master, Wardens, &c. of the Silk Throwsters. In 1661 this company employed above 40,000 persons.

However, the silk industry had not really begun in earnest until after the Revocation of the Edict of Nantes. This was over 400 years after the Crusaders had brought silk-manufacturing knowledge to Italy and the English silk industry was still very much in its infancy by comparison with Italy. The Revocation of the Edict of Nantes in 1685 by Louis XIV ended religious toleration once more for the Protestant Huguenots of Catholic France and thousands more fled to England bringing with them their silk-weaving skills and their experience in sericulture. This time, many of them settled in the Spitalfields area of London, but a number travelled to the north-west where there had been some silk weaving since the reign of Edward III. There were attempts to introduce silkworms and mulberry trees into England, but English sericulture remained difficult because neither the mulberry bushes nor the silkworms were really suited to the English climate.

Refugees fleeing to England from the intolerances of Catholicism was ironic since James II, the king in 1685, was said to be secretly of the Catholic faith, although outwardly he upheld the Protestant faith because Catholicism was still illegal in England. James had two daughters, Mary and Anne, by his Protestant first wife, Anne Hyde. In 1677, their daughter, Mary, married her cousin, William III of Orange. After Anne Hyde's death, James II remarried, but his new wife, Mary of Modena, was an Italian Catholic princess, and, in 1688, when she gave birth to a son, the English Protestant hierarchy became seriously alarmed. Consequently, they invited Mary and her husband, William, to reign as joint monarchs in place of Mary's father, James II. Upon their acceptance, James and his new family fled to France. This became known as the 'bloodless revolution' and, through William, introduced a strong Dutch element into English affairs. The Dutch already had silk-throwing machinery, but this was of inferior quality to the Italian silk-throwing machines.

In 1692, a small group of people applied to form a company for the purpose of starting a silk mill with, it is said, Italian machinery. Judging from John Lombe's later experience this sounds unlikely but, in any case, the application was unsuccessful. It may simply have been a type of machinery similar to that of the Italians. The National Archives hold the records of a case involving Clarke versus Pilkington, initiated by a Bill of 1692 for 'Letters Patent granted for an invention for winding and throwing silk'. However, in 1693, Thomas Pilkington, a London merchant, decided he wanted to sell his shares in this invention, but he was legally challenged by two plaintiffs, Francis Clarke, a tailor, and Isaac Loader, a merchant, who may indeed have been the invention's creators.

The importation of silk was still causing problems, however. In November 1692 a Petition of the Turkey Governor and Company of Merchants of England trading into the Levant Seas was read; setting forth,

> That a Bill being brought into the House for the Importation of the *Italian*, *Sicilian,* and *Naples* Thrown

Silk, notwithstanding an Act made by this Parliament to the contrary, to good Effect; the Petitioners conceive the said Bill is very prejudicial to the Exportation of the Woolen Manufacture, and the Art of Throwing Silk; a discouragement to Navigation, and the trading Subjects of this Kingdom; whereby Trade will inevitably fall into the Hands of the *Dutch*, and other Foreigners: And praying to be heard against the said Bill. *Ordered,* That the said Petition do lie upon the Table, until the said Bill be read the Second time.

(*House of Commons Journal* Volume 10:
22 November 1692 pp. 709–10)

By 1700, there were small workshops and manufactories turning out woven silks, but they could not compete with the fine quality French or Italian silks which were much in demand. Spitalfields weavers specialised in the manufacture of lustrings (cloth with a glossy finish) and alamode (a plain simple tabby weave) silks. In 1692, the Spitalfields workers had been incorporated into the Royal Lustring Company. This company had then obtained parliamentary legislation to prevent the import of similar products from France on the grounds that the company's products were of greater quality. The company thrived initially, but imports from France continued, often through smuggling, so in 1698 the company charter was confirmed by an Act of Parliament which extended its 'powers and privileges'. In effect this meant 'the sole right of making, dressing and lustrating of plain and black alamodes and lustrings' for a period of fourteen years. However, the company failed before the fourteen-year period ended in 1712. French imports had continued and in 1713 silk weavers presented a further petition to parliament concerning the problem of silk imports as per the commercial treaty with France stating that:

by the encouragement of the Crown and divers Acts of Parliament, the silk manufacture is come to be twenty times as great as it was in the year 1664, and that all sorts of good black and coloured silks, gold and silver stuffs and ribands, are now made here as in France. the black silk for hoods and scarves, not made here above twenty-five years ago, hath amounted annually to £300,000 [around £63 million in modern values] for several years past, which before were imported from France. Which increases of the silk manufacture hath caused an increase in our exportation of woollen goods to Turkey, Italy &c.

However, change was in the air and this time was just a lull, the fake calm, before the storm of mechanised innovation and production which broke over the unsuspecting pretty green fields of Britain. England, in fact, was on the cusp of major changes. In 1714, Queen Anne died leaving no heirs, and the crown passed into German royal hands. The main Stuart line had failed but Sophia, a cousin of James II and Charles II, had married the Elector of Hanover, and their son became George I of England. The new king did not speak English and did not want to be in England at all, but gradually he bowed to the inevitable and consoled himself by scoffing English puddings in great quantities. Neither George I, nor his son, George II, were ever properly Anglicised, and this situation did not really change until the accession of George III in 1760.

Chapter 7

The English Industrial Revolution from 1700 onwards

In 1720, England was rocked by the South Sea Bubble scandal which precipitated an economic crisis, the like of which would not be seen again for 300 years. The South Sea Company, formed in 1711, initially under the auspices of fisheries, mainly traded in slaves with Spanish America. The company hoped for more favourable economic conditions after the Treaty of Utrecht in 1713 ended the War of the Spanish Succession, but this did not happen. An annual tax was levied on imported slaves so the company was further limited in its trading facilities. In 1718, George I, sensing an opportunity to make himself a fast buck, had become the governor of the South Sea Company which was then subsequently granted a monopoly on supplying African slaves to South America and the South Sea islands. In 1720, the company offered to underwrite the national debt in return for this exclusive trading monopoly. This created huge confidence in the company, greatly increasing its stock values. Share prices soared and everyone rushed to buy them. The expectation of the profits from the slave trade were heavily promoted but over exaggerated, and, as a result, trading prices far exceeded the actual profits. In addition, there was a great deal of insider trading, corrupt financial practice and bribery to ensure the passing of Acts of Parliament necessary to support the South Sea Company. It could not last and finally the 'Bubble' collapsed spectacularly, ruining thousands in the process.

The episode of John Lombe's industrial espionage in Italy, and the passing of the patents for his new silk-throwing machinery patent in 1718, may well have been overshadowed by these events. However, parliament saw no reason at the time not to grant him and his brother, Thomas, a monopoly on the use of the new machinery which put others involved in the silk industry at a distinct disadvantage. Fashions, however, were as fickle in the eighteenth century as they are today. Silk was a smooth, beautiful, often brilliantly coloured, fabric with a soft luxurious touch that caressed the skin. Although much coveted, silk was expensive and ordinary working people simply could not afford it. However, the East India Company rule in the Indian sub-continent would change all that. The Company was originally incorporated on 31 December 1600 for trade with India, east and south-east Asia, primarily in spices and salt at the time; by 1757, the Company was exercising military rule in India which would last until the establishment of the Raj in 1858. Company trade had also increased to include tea and textiles, saltpetre for gunpowder and opium. Silk was imported from India, so too were Indian cottons, cheaper and more durable than silk, both in white and brilliant colours, which rapidly became very popular. Consequently, during the latter part of the eighteenth century, silk began to decline in popularity as demand grew for the new Indian cottons.

The eighteenth century was also a century of exceptional innovative mechanical inventions; by the 1770s the cotton-manufacturing textile millscape was beginning to emerge in Britain, the first satanic mills starting to appear in England's green and pleasant land, heralding a new era both of great wealth and great poverty.

Why did the major industrial revolution of the late eighteenth century take place in England rather than on the Continent? It is a question often asked. Design? Chance? Fate? It was a mixture. A question of the right place at the right time. At the time, England was a wealthy country with a colonial empire. There were more than adequate financial resources for investing in new industries and there were swathes of empty open countryside on which to build. In addition, there was a sufficient water supply, as well as plenty of coal seams that would later develop into a lucrative mining industry; both provided endless power supplies. One of the main reasons for the north-west of England becoming a major centre for textile production was the abundance of water for water-powered machinery combined with the moist air – caused by frequent heavy rainfall – which prevented threads from becoming brittle and snapping. There was plenty of labour too. The English Agricultural Revolution of the eighteenth century had changed farming methods, used for centuries, to produce more food.

The most important aspects involved selective breeding of cattle and crop rotation, and in 1701 an Oxfordshire farmer, Jethro Tull, had developed an effective horse-drawn seed-drill which sowed seeds in straight rows – a more economical and productive process than the usual scattering of seeds by hand. Methods of surface and sub-surface drainage of farmland were also improved and use of land became far more efficient. The result was a sizeable increase in food supplies which, in turn, resulted in an increase in the population, from 5.5 million in 1700 to 9 million by 1800. There was insufficient work on the land to support this increased population and the surplus numbers would provide a ready pool of workers for the mills. Agricultural wages were traditionally low so many more were enticed away by the promise of better opportunities and better wages in the urban manufactories.

The British Industrial Revolution changed the face of the world and the course of history. England claimed the credit for the instigation and inventions of this period, duly reaping the rewards, and it is generally regarded as the first industrial revolution, but it certainly wasn't the first one – just the first one to begin on English soil. It did not begin with the cotton mills of the north-west, as popularly supposed, but grew from the manufacture of a rival textile on the banks of the River Derwent in Derbyshire half a century earlier; although it has to be remembered that the real story had not begun in England's green and pleasant land at all, but in Italy, during the time of the fabled Knights Templar, and it was simply the first part of this story which ended in Derbyshire 500 years later.

Chapter 8

The English Silk Industry and the Lombe Family

It is tempting to wonder why Derbyshire should be chosen for the initiation of a modern and successful silk-manufacturing industry. Many of the specialist silk workers had settled in Spitalfields in London; there was a large contingent in Wiltshire centred on Malmesbury; there were a number settled in or near Manchester and also in the south-west; yet the man who brought successful silk organzine manufacturing to England was the son of a Norfolk worsted woollens weaver. Fate, rather than geographical location, seems to have determined the exact location of where the Industrial Revolution on textiles should actually begin. The main qualification was that it was necessary to be close to a river for the necessary water power. The link appears to be John Lombe's eldest brother, Thomas. Their father had died when Thomas was still a child so when he became a teenager he went to London in search of an apprenticeship and found one as a mercer, a dealer in textile fabrics, especially silks and velvets. This would have been around the same time that Thomas Cotchett was starting to build his silk mill in Derby. John was about 10 when Cotchett's mill first began silk production in 1703. Thomas Lombe already knew that silk was a popular investment industry and, as part of his job, he would certainly have sourced the new mill for its organzine output. While doing so, he may have seen the opportunity of an apprenticeship for John. What is known is that John worked there for several years until the mill failed around 1713. The reason for the failure was that the Dutch silk-throwing machinery that Cotchett had installed was slower and less reliable than the Italian silk-throwing machinery. The Italians had cornered the market in organzine thread of quality, produced efficiently and effectively, but this came at quite an expensive price – far too high for many. John was interested in mechanics and had proved himself to be quite an able engineer, but he lost his job when the mill closed; he brooded deeply over the fact that, because the Italians refused to share the secrets of their silk-throwing success, it meant that the production of silk thread from other countries, especially England, remained inferior to Italian organzine. There was no reason why the Italians should have shared their silk-throwing secrets and put themselves at a commercial disadvantage, but John Lombe did not see it that way. He was furious and resentful at what he considered the mean refusal of the Italians to share, so, consequently, he could not accept the reasons for their actions. From that viewpoint it was not a big step to what he saw as a logical conclusion. If the Italians could not, or would not, share their silk-manufacturing secrets, then he would go to Italy and obtain for himself what was necessary to recreate the Italian methods of silk throwing in England. However, he needed financial backing, so he approached Thomas with his ideas. Thomas proved as enthusiastic about the project as John, and the brothers devised a plan. John would travel to Leghorn (now known as Livorno), ostensibly to source further silk supplies for Thomas. While there, he would look round and assess the opportunities to gain access to the silk-throwing machinery. John was sufficiently accomplished as an engineer and draughtsman to know that he could draw plans of any machinery detailed enough to reproduce that machinery once safely home in England. Thomas would finance his travelling expenses and, if John was successful in obtaining plans and reconstructing the silk-throwing machinery, Thomas would then engage George Sorocold, who had built Thomas Cotchett's silk mill on the banks of the Derwent, to build a second silk mill, adjacent to Cotchett's ruined mill. Thomas Cotchett had died in 1714 which removed potential problems with the location. The die was cast.

Thomas Cotchett

Cotchett was born around 1677 in the village of Mickleover near Derby. His father, Robert, had been an officer in Cromwell's army during the Civil War. The young Thomas had a comfortable upbringing in what is now known as the Old Hall on Orchard Street, built during the time his father spent serving Cromwell. When Thomas grew up he became a qualified solicitor, but, attracted by the commercial profits in silk weaving, he decided, in 1703, that he would build his own small silk mill on the banks of the River Derwent in Derby. Silk twisting was traditionally done by hand in England, but hand processes were slower and produced a less consistent quality of silk. Cotchett's aim was to have raw silk twisted into silk thread using a new innovation of water-powered throwing machinery, thereby hoping to increase quantity and quality which could compete with the fineness of Italian silk. The mill was built by a young local engineer, George Sorocold, who also designed and built a 13.5ft (4.1m) diameter waterwheel to supply the water power. Dutch machinery was installed, and the little mill began production by the side of the quiet but fast-flowing River Derwent. Thomas Cotchett employed local workers to work the mill and among them was another young engineer named John Lombe. The saying that 'all actions have consequences' was never more appropriate for it was John Lombe who would change the face of British industrial textile production.

The stress and humiliation of his silk mill failure in 1713, which had practically bankrupted Cotchett, took its toll on his health and he died later that year. Cotchett wrote his will in 1712, but although probate was granted in 1714 there was little left and this did not help any of his employees who lost their livelihoods as a result of the silk mill closing down.

Thomas Lombe

Thomas Lombe, born in Norwich in 1685, was the eldest of the four sons of Henry Lombe, a worsted weaver who came from a family of silk and woollen weavers in the flat Norfolk countryside around Norwich. Henry Lombe had married twice, and each wife had borne him two sons. Thomas and Henry were the sons of Henry's first wife, Margaret. John Lombe, and his brother, Benjamin, who died in childhood, were the children of Henry's second wife, Willmott. Thomas was apprenticed to Samuel Totton, a London mercer (cloth merchant), and became a member of the Mercers Company in 1707 as well as a freeman of the City of London to which he had moved and where he would spend most of his life. By 1715, Thomas was doing well in business and he had an agent in Leghorn (Livorno) from whom he imported silk, so it would be to Thomas that John turned for financial help with his plans. From 1717 until the 1720s, Thomas was heavily involved with the Derby Silk Mill project and, in 1727, he was made a knight of the realm and he became Sheriff of London, both of which posts would have carried great influence in eighteenth-century London. He died in 1739 leaving a fortune to his wife and two daughters.

John Lombe

John Lombe was born in 1693 to Henry and Willmot Lombe. As custom dictated, Henry Lombe had left his business to Thomas, the eldest son of himself and his first wife. By the time John was in his twenties, Thomas was quite a wealthy businessman and able to finance John's expedition to Italy. Once there, John would try and obtain some work at one of the silk mills, giving him the opportunity to see the methods and types of machinery used for silk production. Then he would secretly draw the machines in sufficient detail so that they could be copied and rebuilt once he was back in England. It was a risky plan but the rewards it promised were great. Thomas agreed to finance him and John set sail for the Florence port of Livorno in 1715.

Piedmont, in 1720, was described as 'a backward state' when its ruler, the Duke of Savoy, also became the King of Sardinia. The silk industry was in decline in this part of northern Italy surrounded by the Alps, but, in any case, Piedmont had specialised in velvets, often with gold or silver threads running through the material, rather than the organzine that John Lombe needed to obtain. Florence 'was the principal seat of the silk manufacturers and the production of organzine'. *Handbook of Florence and its Environs* (Murray, 1861) offers a glimpse of Florence before the destruction and rebuilding of much of the city when it replaced Turin as Italy's capital in 1865:

> the two markets, the Mercato Vecchio and the Mercato Nuovo stand in the neighbourhood of the Piazza del Gran Duca, in the very centre of the ancient Primo Carchio. They are surrounded by narrow streets and exhibit provisions and goods of every kind … the silk looms in Florence are in the houses of the respective weavers.

The silk industry had continued to flourish after John Lombe's time for Murray's guide continues: 'there are silk works at Prato, Siena, Modigliani, Pistoia and Leghorn.'

Prato, famous for manufacturing Turkish Levantine caps, is a township some 10 or 11 miles (17 km) north-west of Florence and was a part of the Florence province until 1992, 'has about thirty manufactories', so much of the mechanical business of throwing, twisting and weaving was done in Prato and the other towns mentioned.

The waters of history have been muddied by a misunderstanding that John Lombe worked in a Piedmont silk mill. Genoa is the nearest large port to Piedmont, but it is known that John Lombe sailed to and from Livorno because his brother's agent, Samuel Lloyd Glovere Urwin, was a silk exporter in the town. The journey to Piedmont from Livorno is quite long (254 miles or 409km), and difficult enough in the twenty-first century, so it is almost inconceivable that John Lombe would have attempted it on the even worse eighteenth-century roads. If he had been going to Piedmont, he would have sailed to Genoa only 117 miles (188km) distant, especially as he knew he might have to leave Italy in a hurry. Besides, he had no reason to go to Genoa, so sailing to Genoa to source silks when Florence was a major centre just 56 miles (90km) from Livorno might have aroused suspicions about an ulterior motive for his visit. In any case, the silk industry of northern Italy was in general decline by this time. Sailing to Livorno to work in a silk mill in Piedmont simply did not make sense.

Prato today has several museums, including one devoted to the history of textiles, and it was in the Museo del Tessuto di Prato, in the shadow of the Castello dell' Imperatore (built for Frederick II of Italy soon after the Crusades), that the answer to this mystery lay. The museum has a photograph on public display captioned 'A Piedmont Silk Mill'. Further research discovered that the term 'Piedmont Silk Mill' refers to a type of silk-throwing machinery which can be worked by one or two people and is often housed in a small structure similar to that of a windmill or watermill. It therefore seemed perfectly possible for John Lombe to have worked in a Piedmont silk mill in the Florence township of Prato, and not in Piedmont. However, silk-producing areas in

Italy had evolved their own silk-throwing machinery and the two chief models appear to have been the Bolognese silk mill and the Milanese silk mill. The image of a silk mill in the Prato museum and the drawing of a silk mill in di Zonca's book strongly resemble the Bolognese silk mill model. Bologna is only 67 miles (108km) from Florence but it is indeed entirely possible that the Prato image was of silk machinery which may have originally been worked in Piedmont.

Florence was an exciting and beautiful place to visit in the eighteenth century. The Renaissance had prompted a surge in literary, artistic, musical and scientific developments, while the city's economy was built on banking and the luxury Italian silk industry. Opera evolved here in the 1590s. Florentine art and architecture were beyond comparison. Even in the twenty-first century, places like the Duomo and the Uffizi still have the power to render people speechless with the beauty, colour, magic and perfection of their creation. The old Piazza del Mercato Vecchio and rows of medieval houses were still in existence in the eighteenth century, adding to the feeling of history and continuity around the city. Florence was then ruled by the powerful Medici family and John Lombe arrived during the waning years of Cosimo III's reign. During his sojourn in Italy, he accepted Florentine hospitality, making friends, drinking the very palatable Tuscan wines, enjoying traditional gnocchi, an enthusiasm for tomato-based dishes, and the newly arrived delicacy of pasta from Arabia. It is tempting to wonder what his thoughts were as he gazed around the beautiful ancient city, at its people going about their business, and his new friends, knowing that he had come on a mission to steal their precious secrets. Did he ever feel remorse or guilt knowing that he would plunder their lovely city and betray their trust, or was he simply interested only in feathering his own nest?

Somewhere along the way John Lombe met an attractive Italian girl. Her name, who she was, where she came from, have been lost to history. Even the nature of their relationship is uncertain, but it is known that she later came to visit him in England. There is no mention of a family member or a chaperone accompanying her, although there is little question, at this period in history, that a pretty unmarried girl would not have been unaccompanied. However, there is not a hint anywhere of a companion. John Lombe never married and there is no record of any betrothal, so the nature of their relationship and her reason for coming to England are as much a mystery as her name and her background.

The exact details of John Lombe's time in Italy have not survived, either in Italy or in England, no doubt due to the great secrecy which shrouded his Italian project, although it is known that he remained in Italy for a year or so and that he was employed in the silk industry for a while. It would have taken some time to gain the trust of his colleagues and employers. However, he managed to persuade a couple of Italian workers to help him in his quest, so he must have talked about it, which would have been a dangerous thing to do. Why he did so and how he convinced them to help him are also lost to history. He may have needed access to one of the silk mills in order to draw plans of the machinery because it is inconceivable the mills would have been left untended or unlocked when they were not in use. In return he may well have simply promised a better life in England for anyone who helped him. Although John Lombe managed to secretly draw the silk-throwing machinery in some detail, local suspicions were finally aroused, and in 1717 he was forced to flee for his life, together with the two Italian workers who had helped him. There is a romantic cloak and dagger story that Lombe and his two helpers were hotly pursued by their Italian colleagues and rode at great speed to Livorno where they managed to obtain passage on an English ship which was just leaving the harbour. The pursuing Italians gave chase, but their own ships were bigger and far less manoeuvrable, so they were simply outsailed by the quicker and more nimble English ship. For John Lombe it had been a lucky escape. On his return to England, John and his brother Thomas put the rest of their plan into action.

By 1719, the first fully recorded act of industrial espionage had been successfully completed and the new silk mill was flourishing. The Italians were outraged and horrified when they discovered that the precious secrets of their silk-throwing machinery had been stolen and it caused a very serious diplomatic incident. Not only had the British stolen their most cherished silk trade secrets but they were now producing organzine of equal or better quality, and often more cheaply. It resulted in a huge row between England and Italy, after which the Italians refused for some time to export any more raw silk to England and set about plotting their revenge. The Medici of Florence were bitterly angry but, for their own political reasons, they did not wish to offend England terminally. Cosimo de Medici was nearing the end of his life and was beset by problems, mostly of his own creation, caused by his extreme piety, the over-zealous 'moral laws' he instituted, the huge fines he imposed on those for not abiding by his 'moral laws', as well as the crippling taxes and tariffs which he instigated, all of which severely punished the economy of Florence and Tuscany.

However, His Royal Highness, Vittorio Amadeus, King of Sardinia and Prince of Piedmont, had no such scruples. Piedmont had once had an important silk industry, although, by now, it was in decline, and he feared that the remaining silk manufactories in Piedmont would suffer even further as a result of Lombe's actions. He was also greatly offended by England's presumption that Italy's trade secrets could simply be stolen for its own benefit. Therefore, he decided, an example had to be made – but at this point the historical record becomes murky. Unsurprisingly, because if revenge was to be taken it had to be done in the utmost secrecy. Although it was 100 years before the emergence of the mafia in Italy, court intrigues have existed throughout history. The fact that John Lombe's mystery lady could afford to visit him meant that either she was not poor or that she was being well paid to do so, which is what Vittorio Amadeus may discreetly have done, especially if she had been as offended as the king by Lombe's actions. While any actual connection between the Sardinian king and this mystery woman is unknown, it was certainly not impossible. The silence of the Italian historical record matches that of the English historical record, but, given the nature of the situation, this would not be unusual. However, in Derby there were whispered stories and suspicions, and a feeling that something was not right after John Lombe's premature death.

There is always a grain of truth in folk tales and it is a matter of trying to decide what that truth is. From contemporary records there is little doubt that, either late in 1721 or early in 1722, an attractive Italian lady did arrive in Derby and that she was not a stranger to John Lombe. Whether she was related to the Italian workers who came to Derby with Lombe when he escaped from Italy is not known either, but there were rumours that she knew at least one of them well enough. John Lombe clearly trusted her because he made no attempt to avoid her, and he was seen in her company on several occasions. There were even whispers of a romance although there is no evidence at all for this supposition. However, why would an attractive young lady leave her own warm and colourful country of Italy for the foreign dampness and dismal fogs of Derbyshire? In the eighteenth century, when women still faced so many restrictions in all aspects of their lives, romance has to be a strong contender for the reason. The Sardinian king would have been well aware of this fact, and he would also have realised that a mere woman would create far less suspicion than a man. The only other plausible explanation might be that she was presented as a female relative of an Italian whom John Lombe knew and that he agreed to keep an eye on her while she visited Derby, perhaps to see friends or other relatives. There is no written record but the lack of confirming correspondence could be due to language difficulties or the need for secrecy. What is certain is that John Lombe died unexpectedly at the early age of 29, on 20 November 1722, after a painful illness of unknown origin. Conspiracy theories abounded, but they were not entirely without foundation. There is little doubt that he was poisoned, a fact which was medically confirmed at the time, but how or by whom remains a mystery. John Lombe was buried at All Saints, Derby, now Derby Cathedral. The funeral procession was the largest ever seen in Derby, stretching and curling its way around several streets. According to Will Hutton:

> John Lombe's [funeral] was the most superb ever known in Derby. A man of peaceable deportment, who had brought a beneficial manufactory into the place, employed the poor, and at advanced wages, could not fail meeting with respect, and his melancholy end with pity. Exclusive of the gentlemen who attended, all the people concerned in the works were invited. The procession marched in pairs, and extended the length of Full Street, the market-place, and Iron-gate; so that when the corpse entered All Saints, at St. Mary's Gate, the last couple left the house of the deceased, at the corner of Silk-mill Lane.

John Lombe's death was even reported in the London newspapers.

> We hear from Derby, that the whole Town are in Tears for the Death of the most ingenious Mr. John Lombe, the youngest of the two Brothers, who have lately set up a manufacture in this Town for the making of Italian Fabricated Silk ... this ingenious Gentleman having spent some time in Italy, with great Expence and Hazard of his Person, had made himself entirely Master of this valuable Art, and in Conjunction with his Brother Mr. Thomas Lombe, has erected a large Fabrick in this

Town, where some Hundreds of poor People, chiefly Women and Children, are now employ'd, and it is to be hoped will continue to be so by the Surviving Brother.

(*The Post Boy* 22 November 1722)

John Lombe had been a fit young man but he spent the last year of his life suffering from an unidentified stomach ailment. His doctor suspected that he might have been poisoned but, in the days before forensic science, evidence of this was purely circumstantial. Those close to John, including the Italian lady, were questioned. Although grieving, his friends were co-operative but no definite proof of a crime could be ascertained. The mourners who attended John Lombe's funeral were too numerous to be named individually, but it is virtually certain that the Italian lady and Lombe's two Italian workers attended because their absence would have been noted as unusual. Soon after the funeral the Italian lady disappeared. A contemporary Derby citizen remarked that one morning she just wasn't there. The most likely explanation is that she returned to Italy but for that she would have needed help, and once again, the shadowy figure of the Sardinian king hovers in the background, even though there is no hard evidence that he was in any way involved. Someone must have known who she was. John Lombe undoubtedly did, and he must have introduced her to his brothers and to other people because she remained in Derby for about a year. It also appears likely that the two Italian workers who came to England with John Lombe also knew who she was, but any knowledge was taken with them to their graves. This begs the question as to why her name has remained shrouded in such secrecy.

The bitter irony was that John Lombe had never even needed to leave English shores in order to achieve his ambitions. On the shelves of the Bodleian Library in Oxford is a book by Vittorio di Zonca, first published in 1607, again in 1627, and republished at Padua in 1656, *Novo Teatro di Machine et Edificii per uarie et sicure operation.* The medieval Italian does not translate easily but basically it is a book of new machines, buildings and inventions in full detail with drawings of their construction. The plans, drawn by Zonca, of silk winding, spinning and twisting machinery, for which John Lombe paid with his life, were available in England all the time, but, in the days before widespread literacy, public libraries, social media and online technology, he would have no way of knowing that. However, Derby Silk Mill prospered.

Scottish writer and campaigner, Samuel Smiles, in his book *Men of Invention and Industry* (1894. Ch. IV) states that 'enough thrown silk was manufactured to supply the trade, and the weaving of silk became a thriving business'. Indeed, English silk began to have a European reputation. In olden times it was said that 'the stranger buys of the Englishman the case of the fox for a groat [4*d*] and sells him the tail again for a shilling.' But now the matter was reversed, and the saying was: 'The Englishman buys silk of the stranger for twenty marks and sells him the same again for one hundred pounds.'

Henry Lombe

Henry Lombe was born in Norfolk in 1686. Very little is known about him except that he worked with his brothers, Thomas and John. John's untimely death in 1722 was followed by a further mysterious episode and another strange and unexpected death. Thomas Lombe had spent most of December 1722 inducting Henry Lombe, this largely forgotten middle brother, 'with every part of the business' and it was clear that Henry would be expected to manage the business in Derby while Thomas lived in London and conducted his own business there. Early in January 1723 Henry Lombe wrote a 'wonderfully descriptive letter' to his brother-in-law about the Derby Silk Mill and his new responsibilities. However, just six months later, in June 1723, Henry Lombe, 'being of a melancholy turn'

(Will Hutton, 1791), shot himself and was buried at St Michael's Church, Derby.

Henry Lombe's untimely death raises some interesting questions. Why did he shoot himself? There is a sense that this middle brother, sandwiched between the rich elder brother and the younger dare-devil brother who had just succeeded in a major coup of international industrial espionage, may have felt that he was simply a tool of convenience to be used by either brother to do the things they did not have the time to do, or did not want to do, and, as such, did he not merit much esteem, or even feel that he was a person in his own right in charge of his own affairs. Possibly the responsibilities of the mill may have proved too much for him, or he just did not want to work in the business. Perhaps he knew more about the mystery Italian lady than he would ever admit. It seems fairly certain, albeit at a distance of 300 years, that Henry Lombe did commit suicide, but at that time suicide was considered a mortal sin, and those who died by their own hand were not allowed to be buried in consecrated ground. They were usually buried outside the churchyard walls. However, those close to Henry insisted that he had simply been under great stress and that his death was just a tragic accident, so his burial within the churchyard of St Michael's Church was permitted. It is strange, however, that with his own death occurring so soon after his brother's death, he was not buried near his brother, John, in All Saints churchyard. After his death, a cousin, William Lombe, took over the management of the silk mill.

Chapter 9

The Lombe Patent of 1719

In the summer of 1718, a lengthy application was granted to Thomas Lombe for a patent (now no. 422 in early patents) for 'three sorts of engines never before made or used within Great Britain, one to wind finest raw silk, another to spin and the other to twist the finest Italian raw silk into organzine in great perfection', which was carefully recorded in Hansard's Parliamentary proceedings. Thomas Lombe openly admitted that he

> brought into this kingdom that of making the three capital, engines or setts of working tools called in Italy *il inganatore* or *incaruator, fillato*, and *iltort*, and all the several parts belonging to them, with all the arts used in, with, or about them to work their fine raw silk in organzine, which are now used in Bologna, Piedmont, Bergamo, Bassan, and all such organzine silks … and these, together with the improvements and additions I have made to them, I declare to be the engines and I proceed to specify and describe several of the principal parts, machines, wheels, and instruments, and their offices and uses, together with the additions and improvements and to adapt and render them as useful in our own country and climate.

It was in fact John Lombe who had done this work, but Thomas Lombe had financed it and he was always keen to point this out when discussing costs and justifying his application for a fourteen-year patent (fourteen years seems to have been the average length of time for which a patent was granted) and an Act whereby he could renew the patent in 1732 when the first patent had expired. Thomas Lombe gave very detailed specifications of the machinery, although these were doubtless drawn up for him by John Lombe. The following is a précis of these specifications since, in the actual text of the patent, there is a good deal of repetition and redundant language as per the customs of the times:

> The first engine [*il inganatore*] to wind the finest raw silk consists of several divisions and receives its original motion from a cog wheel which is communicated to the upright shafts, on all of which are fixed either rounds or heads of cogs, which give motion to the laying shafts, and those to the small uprights of the several divisions of which this engine consists. Each division of the engine receives its own primary motion from a concave wheel, which communicates to the crown or large wheels, which have lesser concave wheels fixed on them, thereby they put forward and also draw back the motion on pulleys. Each of the large concave wheels will give motion to about two hundred and fifty other wheels of various sorts and sizes which work in that division.

Thomas Lombe then goes on to describe how the raw silk is worked by this machine.

> Raw silk is extended and put upon machines called *tavelle* [which have] double arms of wood, with cords and implements to keep them at a proper distance, fixed into blocks of wood with holes in them, upon each of which hangs a small weight to govern the motion. These

machines hang on supporters below the wheels and go round on wires, pins or sticks. Wires put through them and bent down keep them on the more even course and draw the thread straight. The rollers, called *rochito*, upon which the silk winds, have square taper holes through which goes a wooden pin upon which they are turned by wheels, and supported by small boards which have holes for the pins to turn and spare grooves to stop them when the thread is broken. This fine silk is strengthened and preserved from breaking by hot air conveyed by cavities and pipes. Every thread has a holder which guides and holds it over a rail of glass, receives motion from a side wheel, and is carried by a support on rolling pulleys.

It was quite a complicated process but described in a manner that people without engineering experience could follow, and the clarity was appreciated by those trying to understand how the machine worked.

The coupling irons that join the axes, on which the wheels go that are turned by the crown wheels, are in two parts and have rings at one end and holes through near the other [end]. A small implement, by springing up as soon as the thread breaks, stops the roller from going until [the thread] be tied again. Proper places are left to contain the persons that work therein [who] take care of the movements and repairs and all air from breaking the threads or hindering the motions. Irons about eighteen inches long [half a metre], square near the upper end, and pointed at the other end, set in sockets, turned with the hand, and another iron, tapered and pointed towards both ends, with a round piece of iron, four or five inches in diameter on the middle, fixed in a wooden frame which is set on the lap and turned without any wheel, only by rubbing the hand on one side of the iron plate, while the silk winds on the other, are both used to wind it double.

It is quite important to understand the full specification of this machinery because it is such a key factor in the evolution of Arkwright's water frame. Thomas Lombe gave as much detail for the other two 'engines' as he did for the first one.

The engine to spin the raw silk called *fillats* is a machine which receives its motion from the long shafts of timber which turn on gudgeons of steel in brass sockets. The laying shafts are turned by the main uprights or cog wheels and have rounds or heads of cogs fixed on them to tooth in with the great wheel which gives the first motion to this engine, whose middle part turns on the point of a steel gudgeon in a brass pot. The outer parts of this engine consist of upright pillars of wood set [at] about two or three feet distance, which support the work, with wheels and machines. The middle part consists of a large framework of wood (*il arbero*), built on a shaft, with cords, turners' pulleys, and weights fixed thereon and by its own motion turns the principal wheels of the work. The rollers (*rochots*), on which the raw silk is to be spun, are put upon instruments composed partly of lead and iron, have square places in the middle and are round at each end, go in sockets and have holes at the top for wooden pins to go through. Upon these the rollers are turned extremely swift, and on the end of each is a coronet of wood with a hole through the same. The motion of the main middle frame gives motion to the great wheels in each row and the rest of the wheels in the whole engine. A small hand is fixed on a board worked by a side wheel and guides every thread over a glass rail to the receivers (*rochello*) which are on poles of wood (*bachettis*) with wires several together and are turned by wheels. Weights regulate the motions of the rollers … Places are made all about the engine and scaffolds built round it for the persons to stand on that work it. The warm air which preserves the silk [is] brought to it by pipes from the furnace.

The final part of Thomas Lombe's specification was just as detailed as the first two parts.

The third engine, to twist the silk thread into organzine (*il tort*), is either fixed over or under the former [engine] to receive the benefit of the same motion in a very lofty building or separate by itself; in the latter case it receives its motion by a wheel fixed on its shaft above or below it, or by cogs around the whole circumference of the moving part. The outer part has standards, as the *fillats* only may be made more distant, movable and in two lengths; the inner frame also goes round 'serpo' (more slowly or glides), and has large arms for upholders of the long shafts. This movement carries round the capital wheels which turn the rest. The sides of this engine are made to open to take out the organzine silk when done. Here the instruments on which the receivers turn, which have the spun silk upon them, are single, like those of the second engine, made with lead and iron. If the silk be double [then] larger and more weighty; but if the silk is put on here to be made into organzine directly from the second engine, then the iron instrument must have two ends, fork fashion, on each of which can go one of the receivers (*rochottis*) with coronets of wood on their top, and with hands too each hold the thread open. These then pass over a small wire. which, when either of the ends break, breaks the other also. Above there is a hand which receives both the threads together and guides them on to little frames hasps with iron pins and wheels which are fixed one above another, upon which the skeins of organzine are formed, and are soon afterwards made up into knots or hanks by an iron instrument with wheels for that purpose, which, when the designed quality is hanged upon the hook immediately twists it up into the proper form. This engine also receives warm air from a furnace below it.

Thomas Lombe also adds that 'the cog wheels, shafts and original motions aforementioned suppose these engines shall be worked by water … if they were to be used any other way then the original motions may be different.'

One interesting point emerged and that is the use of rollers in the spinning process. John Kennedy, 100 years later, believed that rollers were not used in silk spinning but, in fact, these rollers may have provided the inspiration for John Wyatt and Lewis Paul to develop their own rollers, which, coincidentally, were patented a mere half dozen years after parliament had refused to renew Thomas Lombe's patent in 1732.

Chapter 10

Derby Silk Mill

In 1717, Thomas Lombe had commissioned George Sorocold to build a new silk mill on an island in the Derwent adjacent to Cotchett's failed mill. Sorocold built the new mill in an Italianate style as a tribute to John Lombe. The mill was 33.5m (110ft) long x 12m wide (39ft) x 17m (56ft) high and was built on top of a series of stone arches which allowed the River Derwent to flow beneath. The site was 'entered by a bridge ... with gates made by Robert Bakewell, the prominent Derby wrought-iron smith', and had no fewer than forty-six windows. Sorocold's 7m (23ft) diameter and 2m (6ft 6ins) wide undershot waterwheel provided power for the whole mill. Samuel Smiles later calculated that, together with fixtures, fittings and John Lombe's new machinery, the whole venture had cost them £30,000 (just under £4,500,000 in modern values). The mill also had to be heated for processing of the silk and this was done by a 'fire-engine' which would pump hot air around the building. While the mill was being built, John Lombe rented rooms in Derby Town Hall where he developed the prototype machinery from the drawings he had made in Italy.

An early contemporary description of the silk mill exists, written by Daniel Defoe who visited the Lombe mill during a visit to Derby in the 1720s. He wrote 'this engine contains 25,586 wheels, and 96,746 movements, which work 73,726 yards of silk thread, every time the waterwheel goes round, which it does three times in one minute.' This was followed by another description from someone in the 1740s who wrote that 'the original Italian works of five storeys high housed 26 Italian winding engines that spun raw silk on each of the upper three floors while the lower two storeys contained eight spinning mills, producing basic thread, and four twist mills.'

Dr Samuel Johnson visited the silk mill in 1774 and commented 'I remarked a particular manner of propagating motion from a horizontal to a vertical wheel.' Johnson also understood some of the mechanical processes.

Three years later, in 1777, on Samuel Johnson's advice, James Boswell also visited the mill, noting that 'Mr John Lombe had a patent for having brought away contrivances from Italy … [but I am] … not to think with dejected indifference of the works of art.' Boswell did, however, praise the machinery and 'its multiple operations'.

Samuel Smiles in his book *Men of Invention and Industry* (J. Murray. 1890) wrote:

> at length, after about three years' labour, the great silk mill was completed. It was founded upon huge piles of oak, from 16 to 20 feet long, driven into the swamp close to each other by an engine made for the purpose. The building was five storeys high, contained eight large apartments, and had no fewer than 468 windows. The Lombes must have had great confidence in their speculation, as the building and the great engine for making the organzine silk, together with the other fittings, cost them about 30,000L.

However, the mill had burned down in 1826, and had been rebuilt so Smiles was not viewing the original building. Ironically, in the same year as Smiles' book was published the doubling shop collapsed and also had to be rebuilt. Smiles also quotes Hutton at some length on the story of the Derby Silk Mill but throws in a note of caution. 'Hutton says that he [John Lombe] bribed the workmen; but this would have been a dangerous step, and would probably have led to his expulsion, if not to his execution.'

Although some visitors were impressed by the machinery, the scale and size of this ambitious project, other visitors commented upon the heat, the smell, the noise, and the unhealthy appearance of the child workers in the silk mill.

Will Hutton

It was Will Hutton who really condemned conditions in the silk mill. Hutton, who wrote the *History of Derby* in 1791, included in his book the earliest known fully detailed description of the Lombe mill, the brothers who ran it, the work that was done there and his own experiences as a young child working as an apprentice within the silk mill.

Will Hutton was the son of a local woolcomber. He was born in 1723 and in 1728, at the age of 5, he was sent to school for a couple of years where he learned to read and write. In 1730, when Hutton was 7, his father acquired a seven-year apprenticeship for him at the silk mill.

> My parents, through mere necessity, put me to labour before Nature had made me able. Low as the engines were, I was too short to reach them. To remedy this defect, a pair of high pattens [a type of protective outdoor overshoes] were fabricated, and lashed to my feet, which I dragged after me till time lengthened my stature. The confinement and the labour were no burden; but the severity was intolerable, the marks of which I yet carry, and shall carry to the grave. The inadvertencies of an infant, committed without design, can never merit the extreme of harsh treatment.

He wrote of the long hours, low wages and ill-treatment of children at the mill, before adding

> They were the most unhappy years of my life … the threads were continually breaking and to tie them is principally the business of children whose fingers are nimble.

And if the child was clumsy or simply got it wrong the punishment could be severe. Derby Silk Mill was not alone in the way it treated its child apprentices. This type of treatment was common in all textile mills as late as the 1860s. Some, like Quarry Bank Mill in Cheshire, were more enlightened, allowing their apprentices proper food, an hour of education daily, and the services of a local doctor. In others, such as Samuel Oldknow's mill at Marple, the children worked endlessly in hard, miserable conditions and some drowned themselves in the millpond there rather than face the harsh servitude any longer. In 1832, the novelist Fanny Trollope had noted of Manchester mills that 'factory conditions were incomparably more severe than those suffered by plantation slaves', and commented that 'Hutton had a great detestation of the Lombe silk factory at Derby, where he was employed when a boy, and everything that he says about it must be taken *cum grano salis*.' However, Hutton remains an important source because of his intimate knowledge of the Derby Silk Mill and its owners. It was common knowledge, he said, that the Italians had 'the exclusive art of silk throwing'; consequently, an absolute command of that lucrative traffic. The wear of silks was due to the taste of the ladies, explaining in his *History of Derby* the decision of Mr. Cotchett to enter the business of silk throwing.

> This unfortunate gentleman started a small silk mill at Derby, with the object of participating in the profits derived from the manufacture and the British merchant was obliged to apply to the Italian [merchant] with ready money for the article at an exorbitant price.

Hutton went on to say that Cotchett did not succeed in his undertaking.

> Three engines were found necessary for the process: he had but one. An untoward trade is a dreadful sink for money; and an imprudent tradesman is still more dreadful. We often see instances where a fortune would last a man much longer if he lived upon his capital, than if he sent it into trade. Cotchett soon became insolvent.

In telling the story of the failure of Cotchett's mill, Hutton also tells of John Lombe's reaction.

> John Lombe, a man of spirit, a good draughtsman, and an excellent mechanic, travelled into Italy with a view of penetrating the secret. He stayed some time; but as he knew admission was prohibited, he adopted the usual mode of accomplishing his end by corrupting the servants. This gained him frequent access in private. Whatever part he became master of, he committed to paper before he slept. By perseverance and bribery he acquired the whole, when the plot was discovered, and he fled, with the utmost precipitation, on board a ship, at the hazard of his life, taking with him two natives, who had favoured his interest and his life, at the risk of their own.

One of the two 'natives' was called Nathaniel Gartrevalli who remained in Derby after John Lombe's death. The other was said to have fled with the mystery Italian lady and may have been involved in the poisoning of John Lombe. Hutton knew Gartrevalli but was unimpressed, stating that 'him [Gartrevalli] I personally knew; he ended his days in poverty; the frequent reward of the man who ventures his life in a base cause or betrays his country.'

Considering that Hutton admired John Lombe, and that Gartrevalli had helped Lombe in what Hutton appeared to think was an admirable cause, it was a harsh and perhaps hypocritical judgement. Hutton continues to describe what happened after Lombe's return from Italy. He wasn't even born when John Lombe carried out his act of industrial espionage or when the silk mill was built, but he knew, probably from hearing his father talk about it, that Lombe had taken rooms at Derby Town Hall, during the time between his return to England and the time the mill was ready for business, where he built temporary hand-turned engines to begin his business. However, Hutton dismisses one writer's enthusiastic description of the mill as containing '26,000 wheels, 97,000 movements, which work 71,000 yards of silk thread, while the waterwheel, which is 18 feet high, makes one revolution, and that three are performed in a minute. That one fire-engine conveys warmth and that one regulator governs the whole.'

He bristles at the inaccuracies because he had learned otherwise during his experience as an apprentice at the mill and he corrects the unknown writer. 'If he had paid an unremitting attendance for seven years he might have found their number [of wheels] 13,384 movements … [and] number of yards wound, every circuit of the wheel, no man can tell.'

He dismisses the 'fire-engine' as 'a common stove which warmed one corner of that large building'. The regulator, he says, is 'a peg in the master-wheel which strikes a small bell every revolution: near it is a pendulum which vibrates about fifty times in a minute.'

Hutton also described the silk-throwing and spinning processes in some detail which he would have learned from his time as an apprentice in the silk mill.

> The raw silk is brought in hanks or skeins, called flips, and would take five or six days in winding off, though kept moving ten hours a day. Some are the produce

of Persia; others of Canton, coarse ... some are from China, perfectly white. The work passes through three different engines; one to wind; the second to twist; and the third to double. Though the thread is fine it is an accumulation of many. The workman's care is chiefly to unite, by a knot, a thread that breaks; to take out the burs and uneven parts, some of which are little bags [cocoons] ... The threads are continually breaking; and to tie them is principally the business of children whose fingers are nimble. The machine continually turns around [a] bobbin or small block of wood, which draws the thread from the slip expanded upon a swift, suspended on a centre. The moment the thread breaks, the swift stops. One person commands from twenty to sixty threads, if many cease, at the same time, to turn, it amounts to a fault, and is succeeded by punishment. From the fineness of the materials, the ravelled state of the slips and bobbins, and the imprudence of children, much waste is made, which is another motive of correction; and when correction is often inflicted, it steels the breast of the inflictor.

As Will Hutton actually worked in the silk mill for seven years, he would probably have had the best idea of exactly what machinery was there and little incentive to exaggerate.

Chapter 11

End of the Lombe Monopoly

Thomas Lombe, however, when the patent for his machinery came up for renewal in 1732, had every reason to exaggerate. Sir Thomas, as he was by now, waxed fulsomely to the House of Commons Committee who were to decide if his patent should be renewed after a number of complaints about his monopoly. *The Monthly Intelligencer* for April 1732 and *The Gentleman's Magazine* of September and October 1732 told the story, giving Thomas Lombe their support and getting some of their information wrong (as the media still do 300 years later).

The Monthly Intelligencer decided to rely on Daniel Defoe's figures from the early 1720s for the number of wheels, movements and yards of silk thread worked on each revolution of the waterwheel. Will Hutton was only 9 at the time of the application for an extension of the patent, but if the *Intelligencer*'s writer had actually visited the mill any of the workers could have told him that the number of wheels was only half that recorded by Defoe and this would also have considerably affected the number of movements and the yards of silken thread quoted by Defoe.

The Gentleman's Magazine for September 1732 reported the wording of the actual application submitted by Sir Thomas:

> That his late Majesty [George I who had died in 1727] had granted him a patent for the sole making and using of the said engines [descriptions attached to the application see pp. x] for the term of fourteen years; but that several years of the said term were expired before

he could finish it, and by reason of other difficulties
the whole term was expired before he could bring the
manufacture to perfection; therefore prayed the House
is to grant him a further term, or such other recompense
or relief, as to the House should seem meet [*sic*].

The seconder of this application, referred to only as Mr O----pe,
then stated 'That since the petitioner had introduced the most useful
manufacture, he ought to meet with encouragement; that one engine
was set up at Derby, by which that whole county was improved, and
the poor employed. Therefore, he seconded the motion.'

A description of the mill, written between 1739 and 1753
belies the notion that there was only one engine and is supported
by the number of wheels surmised by Daniel Defoe in the early
1720s, and also the number counted by Will Hutton during his
apprenticeship (1730–1737). The other argument against the
venture still remaining an ongoing development in 1732 is the lack
of physical involvement by the Lombe family after 1723. John
Lombe, who may have been still working on possible extensions
of the business, had died in November 1722. Henry Lombe shot
and killed himself in June 1723. Thomas Lombe then appointed
a mill manager and was infrequently seen in Derby, despite the
success of the mill.

The Gentleman's Magazine for October 1732 enlarged on the
details and the discussions. According to Sir Thomas, the initial
reason for the enterprise had been cost 'being sensible that this
nation purchased organzine at a great charge from Savoy, where it
was all made by means of a large and curious engine; they resolved
to bring it hither, though the King of that country had made the
discovery of it [punishable by] immediate death'. Savoy is in
the north of Italy at the northern boundary of the principality of
Piedmont, but Sir Thomas was importing his silk through Livorno,
the nearest port to Florence, and it is known that John Lombe sailed

to Livorno. Villefranche was the main port of Piedmont in the 1700s and Genoa, in the Republic of Genoa next door to Piedmont, was the largest port in the area and served the Duchy of Milan. However, even today, the journey between Villefranche, Genoa and Livorno is long, tedious and difficult. It would have been plainly illogical to have even attempted it in the early eighteenth century, especially by someone fleeing for their life. The conclusion must be, therefore, that much, if not all, of his silk yarn purchase would have come from Florence in the Grand Duchy of Tuscany.

Then the magazine's narrative goes into overdrive:

> After his [John's] return Sir Thomas obtained a patent in 1718. The engine is so large, and there are so many wheels, motions and spindles, and other things that it was three years before he could finish it. When finished, he could make no benefit of it til he procured and instructed a number of persons to work it. Before he could do this his Sardinian Majesty [the King of Savoy had also recently become King of Sardinia] was informed that the engine was set up in England, and immediately prohibited the exportation of silk [yarn] out of his country.

The truth is that the king was worried because the silk trade was declining in many areas of Italy and only Lucca, Florence and Venice were doing sufficient business.

'Before Sir Thomas could get a sufficient quantity stole[*sic*] from thence, the term of his patent was within a few years of being expired; and therefore it was impossible he could as yet have got sufficient recompence.'

Cotchett's mill closed down in 1713 and John Lombe sailed for Italy around 1715. Both brothers were intelligent and experienced in the silk industry. It is unlikely they would not have foreseen such issues and they had almost two years to consider and plan their venture.

One of the MPs debating the issue on Sir Thomas's behalf, identified only as Mr B----d, stated that:

> The chief reason why the petitioner has not made much advantage of his invention, is, that no raw silk is proper for his purpose but the Italian, of which he could procure but little. Of Turkey raw silk he finds it impossible to make good organzine. That brought from China will do, but the company keeps it at so high a price that it will not answer … I do not know what this House may judge a proper recompense; however, all possible care ought to be taken to prevent the invention's being carried out of this country … if we can keep our neighbours from stealing it … twill be a great encouragement to our silk-manufacturing trade.

It is as if Sir Thomas were trying to paint himself as the real victim. The brothers must have known that there would be supply problems with Italian silk once it was discovered what had happened. The Italians had never made a secret of the fact that anyone who stole silk trade secrets would face capital punishment so it was hardly likely they would reward a culprit by supplying him with silk yarn to make his own fortune at the expense of the Italian silk trade. It was John and Thomas Lombe who stole, and capitalised upon, the secrets of the Italian silk-throwing machinery and the Italians who naturally felt angry and betrayed. In any case, as Will Hutton says, Chinese and Persian silk was of perfectly good quality and sufficient for the production of organzine. Carriage from these distant parts would have made it more expensive but that is surely something which would have been foreseen. Having said that, 120 years later, the British government would make the same mistakes about alternative sources of cotton supply when the American Civil War forced the cessation of raw cotton exports to Britain. The audacity and irony of claiming that the 'invention' of the machinery should 'not be carried out of this country … if we can keep our neighbours from stealing it', has to be seen in the context of the eighteenth century. It was the first [known] case of industrial espionage and it was, to eighteenth-century eyes, a huge success. Britain was a wealthy country on the brink of building her empire. The country was not a democracy and the upper classes ruled harshly so that those dependent upon them often had little choice and no say in matters. It is a case that one can explain, even if one cannot excuse, the reasons.

On 2 November 1731, a report on Thomas Lombe's petition was prepared and issued by the House of Commons Committee to whom Sir Thomas had submitted his petition in January 1731 for a further fourteen-year patent to be granted on the use of the silk-throwing machinery. The chairman was Alderman Micajah Perry. Thomas Lombe's petition was discussed in detail and witnesses were called to support the application.

Daniel Booth, a silk weaver stated that:

> Fine Italian organzine silk is absolutely necessary to carry on the silk-weaving trade. In times past merchants have been forced to buy this organzine silk worked in Italy. … Since Sir Thomas Lombe set up his engine it has reduced the price of organzine silk and he has bought as good organzine silk made by the petitioner's engine. … There has been a very great increase in silk manufacture of this kingdom since the said engine was erected and the price [of organzine] very much reduced.

Mr Booth added that 'organzine silk cannot be thrown by hand, but is now perfectly done by the petitioner's engine … and organzine silk is absolutely necessary for making the warp of all fine silks.'

He then referred to various items of silk manufacture, showing the committee samples and patterns of silk made by English silk throwers and fine organzine thread made by Sir Thomas's engine, to demonstrate the differences in quality.

Daniel Booth was followed by William Selwyn, a silk trader and importer of Italian organzine silk. He said that:

> he has imported great quantities of Italian organzine silk for many years and has known several mills set up but [none] that could work the said Italian organzine silk to the perfection that Thomas Lombe's engine does ... and there is great profit by bringing over the silk raw and working it into organzine silk in England.

Roger Drake, an Italian merchant, followed this, stating that 'he has bought several quantities of organzine silk in Italy ... that he has seen the said engine, and that there is not such another in England and organzine silk cannot be thrown by any other mill.' He also believed it had helped to lower the price of Italian silk.

Captain Peter Lekeux, a weaver, also said that Thomas Lombe's engine had succeeded in lowering the cost of expensive Italian silks and that the quality of Lombe's silk manufacture was as good as Italian silk manufacture although Lombe's silk production had not been perfected until a couple of years before the presentation of this petition. 'Organzine silk is absolutely necessary to make all sorts of plain and flowered silks, gold and silver silks, and brocades. Without organzine silk, the silk weavers cannot make any piece of silk.'

In addition, it was pointed out that 'the said Thomas Lombe's engine employs our own poor ... making a new manufacture in England, and is of great advantage to the nation.'

The original patent, dated 8 September 1718, was then submitted with the report and the evidence for due consideration of renewal. Sir Thomas also added a translation of the Italian edict 'whereby it appeared that the disclosing, or attempting to discover, anything to the making of the engines, or working the said organzine silk, is by the said law prohibited in Italy, on pain of death.' It might have been expected that he would play down this aspect, but Sir Thomas had read his audience correctly, for 'it further appeared to the Committee, that the said Sir Thomas Lombe has with the greatest hazard and difficulty found those arts, and brought them here to England, and at a very great expense of his own money, and but lately brought the manufacture to perfection.'

The Committee subsequently decided that he deserved their full support and resolved

> that it is the opinion of this Committee, that a further term of years be granted to Sir Thomas Lombe, his executors, administrators and assigns, beyond the term of fourteen years, granted to him by his late Majesty King George, for the sole privilege, power and authority, of exercising, working, making, using, and enjoying, his new invention of three sorts of engines, or machines, found out, brought out into England, and, since the granting of the said patent, erected by the said Sir Thomas Lombe on the River Derwent, in or near the town of Derby, for making organzine silk, and all benefits arising by the said invention.

There was no mention of his dead brother John, who had risked everything to obtain the secrets from the Italians of successful and quality silk throwing, and who had paid the ultimate price for his daring and treachery. In 1727, Thomas Lombe had been knighted and elected Sheriff of London so he was, by now, a wealthy and influential figure in both London and Derby. The initial fourteen-year period of the monopoly was due to expire in 1732, but, by this time, John and Henry Lombe had both been dead for ten years, and the company was being run mainly by a manager. Various vexed representations had been made to parliament about the Lombe monopoly on the new silk-throwing machinery and parliament agreed. Consequently, they refused to grant Thomas Lombe a further exclusive patent for the sole use of the silk-throwing machinery because it was generally felt that the monopoly should cease, so that other manufacturers might benefit as well. Sir Thomas was very handsomely compensated with the sum of £14,000 (the modern-day equivalent of over £2 million), but parliament's decision not to renew the monopoly threw open the doors to the establishment of silk-weaving manufactories in other places.

Above: Arkwright's carding engine at N.W. Museum of Science and Industry. (Courtesy of Manchester Central Library Local Studies Collection)

Below left: Arkwright's spinning jenny c1767. (Courtesy of Manchester Central Library Local Studies Collection)

Below right: Arkwright's water frame, patented in 1769, at N.W. Museum of Science and Industry. (Courtesy of Manchester Central Library Local Studies Collection)

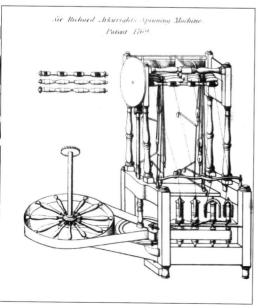

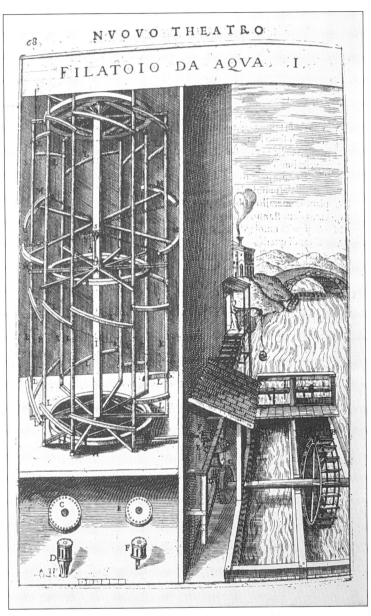

Bolognese water powered silk throwing and spinning machinery developed in the fifteenth-century (Zonca, Vittorio di. 1603) courtesy of Forgotten Books publishing. A Bolognese silk mill 'driven by hydraulic power…has mechanical winders…to automatically perform the spooling operation…and is provided with spools which could give the thread a larger twist angle than reels… the motion… given by the rotation of the water wheel is smoother and more regular…it…was more advanced from a technological point of view than the Milanese silk mill…and the quality of the worked silk…was higher than that produced by the Milanese silk mill…'. (Comino, S. & Gasparetto, A. Silk mills in early modern Italy. Advances in Historical Studies, 9, pp 284-294. 2020)

Right: Castle of Vinci which houses Museo di Leonardo da Vinci and some of his inventions.

Below: Cromford Mill on the River Derwent about 1905. (Courtesy of Derbyshire County Council and Picture the Past)

VIEW FROM HARP EDGE   MATLOCK BATH

Derby Silk Mill on the River Derwent 1925. This is a copy building, not the original buildings which were destroyed twice by fire in the eighteenth and nineteenth centuries.

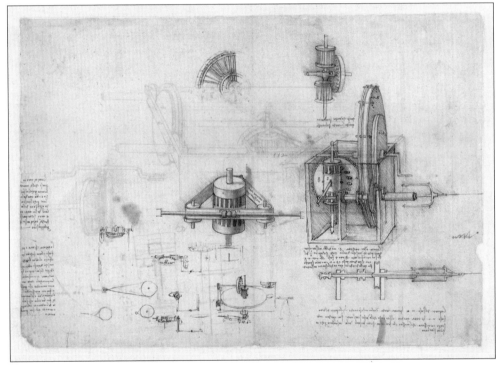

Fin spinner and bobbin winder invented by Leonardo da Vinci (courtesy of Ambrosiana Library Milan). 'one of the most highly innovative machines designed by Leonardo for the manufacturing of textiles…designed to perform the stretching, twisting and winding operations simultaneously on three consecutive stretches of thread…operations which were then repeated as the thread regularly fed into the machine…and was the basis for the later development of the continuous spinning machine…'. (www.museoscienza.org/english/leonardo/fusoaletta.html)

Above: Handspinning in Leigh c1895.
(Courtesy of Manchester Central Library
Local Studies Collection)

Right: Image of Leonardo da Vinci
produced in 1912.

Italian silk throwing mill in Abbadia Lariana (courtesy of Oltre la Valle). An early typical small silk mill.

Lancashire cotton mill interior showing cotton spinning machinery 1920s.

Livorno in 2012, formerly known as Leghorn, and the main port for Florence.

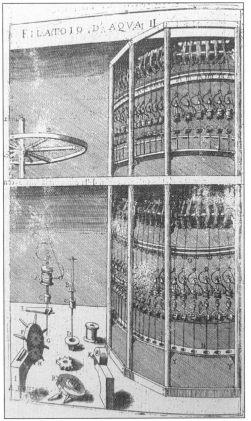

Above: Lucca, where Italian silk manufacture really began, c1920. The tree on top of the medieval tower built as a status symbol (right background) is part of a kitchen garden.

Left: Milanese style horse powered silk throwing and spinning machinery developed in the fifteenth-century machinery (Zonca, Vittorio di. 1603) courtesy of Forgotten Books publishers. 'the Milanese mill is driven by horse or human power…has winders which are operated manually… and reels, not spools. (Comino, S. & Gasparetto, A. Silk mills in early modern Italy. Advances in Historical Studies, 9, pp 284-294. 2020)

Newton Heath Silk Mill built 1852 on Failsworth border. The local railway football team of Newton Heath became Manchester United.

Prato street, c1920s when Prato was known as 'a centre of fashion'.

Shuttles used in the silk industry in Lombardy 1920.

Above left: Silk parachute used in 1943 during the Second World War demonstrating the strength of silk.

Above right: Sir Richard Arkwright c1770. (Courtesy of Manchester Central Library Local Studies Collection)

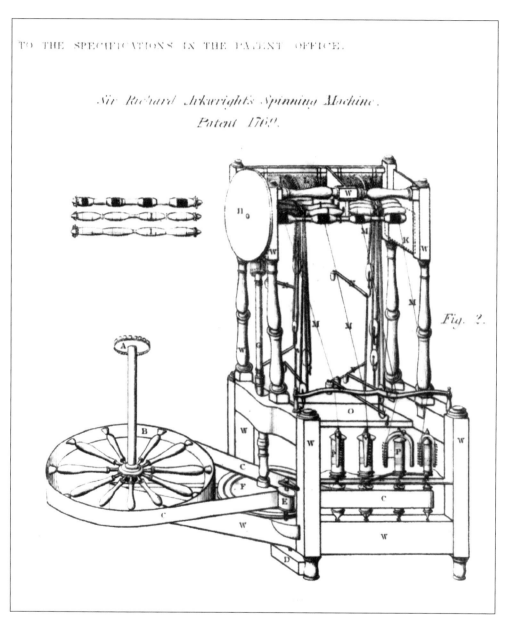

Sir Richard Arkwright's spinning machine patent 1769. (Courtesy of the Patent Office)

St Albans silk mill in c1900. A water-powered silk throwing mill, later powered by steam, built in 1804 by the Woollams family.

Textile mill near Ariano, a town east of Rome. In medieval times Italian textile mills tended to be small affairs no larger than a small windmill or water mill (hence the name), with one or two pieces of machinery, usually powered by water, and worked by two or three people. (The town was notable for the first minting of the ducat (gold coin of current worth £105) by the Sicilian king Roger II in 1140.)

Twyford silk mill 1910, bult by the Billinge brothers in 1798. In 1784 Thomas Billinge was in partnership with Charles Woollam and they called themselves 'silk men.'

View of Vinci from the Castle of Vinci which overlooks the village and houses the Museo di Leonardo.

Vinci. Bronze horse erected on market square as a tribute to Leonardo da Vinci.

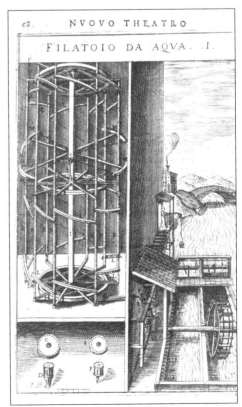

Italian water powered silk throwing and spinning machinery, known as a Bolognese mill, developed in the fifteenth-century, and drawn here by Vittorio di Zonca in 1603.

Woman wearing a cotton dress over a crinoline c1866.

Woman wearing a silk evening gown c1920 showing the smoothness and sheen for which silk is renowned.

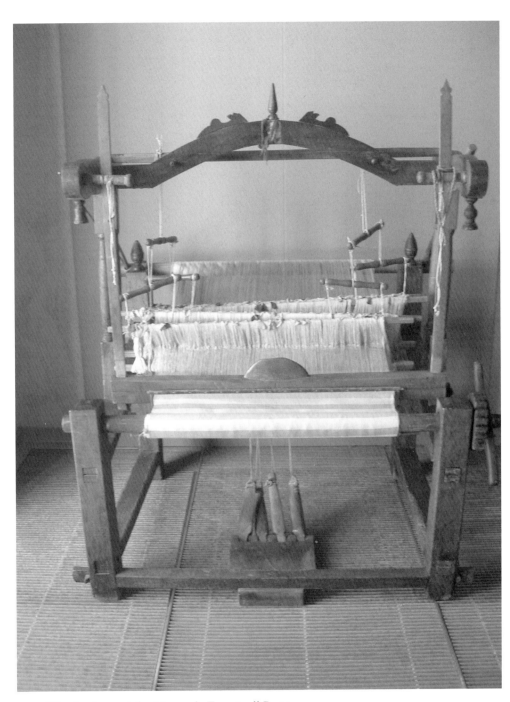

Wooden loom at the Museo de Tessuto di Prato.

Chapter 12

The Eighteenth-Century Silk Industry in England after 1732

There was already a well-established hand-woven silk industry in London around the Spitalfields area, and now new silk mills were established in a number of places in northern England, including: Stockport (Logwood Mill, 1732); Macclesfield (Park Green Mill, 1744 and the Button Mill 1744); Bollington, (Bollington Mill, near Bollington Hall Farm, date uncertain); Congleton (Old Mill, 1753; Dane in Shaw Silk Mill, date uncertain); Leek (had a silk industry dating from the 1670s but most of its silk mills date from the nineteenth century); and Failsworth (Union Mill, date uncertain; Newton Silk Mill 1852). Macclesfield and Bollington specialised in silk buttons; Failsworth in caps and silk hats; Leek specialised in silk buttons and silk ribbons; and Congleton in silk ribbons. There were also silk mills further south, although built at slightly later dates, and those of note included: Malmesbury (built 1793); Twyford (built 1800); St Albans (built 1804); Whitchurch (built 1815); Braintree (first built 1818 and the home of Courtaulds); Sudbury (a number of silk mills but the first one built 1820); Norwich (built 1860 in the home town of the Lombe family). Sudbury initially specialised in parasols and umbrellas, although today there are five silk-manufacturing companies in the town specialising in furnishing fabrics (Gainsborough Silk Weaving who hold a royal warrant); silk ties (Vanners Silks); fashion fabrics and wedding dresses (Stephen Walters, which made wedding dresses for Princess Anne and Princess Diana); high quality furnishing fabrics for palaces and

National Trust properties (Humphries Weaving); jacquard fabrics (Daniel Walters).

A Description of the Countryside from Thirty to Forty Miles around Manchester (Aiken, J. 1795) states that

> the trade of Macclesfield, that of wrought buttons in silk, mohair and twist, is probably its staple. ... The use of them may be traced 150 years backwards ... Macclesfield was always considered the centre of this trade and mills were erected long ago both here and in Stockport for winding silk.

but, at the same time, Aiken noted that

> in Stockport were erected the first mills for winding and throwing silk [after the Derby Silk Mill in 1719], on a plan procured from Italy; and the persons concerned in the silk factories were reckoned the principal people in the place; but on the decline in the trade the machinery was applied to cotton spinning.

His assessment was at odds with Samuel Smiles' assertion that silk production increased and, according to Smiles, the number employed in the silk-manufacturing trade had risen to over a million by 1850. The truth lies somewhere in between. Cotton production, which really began in the early 1770s, was scarcely out of its infancy when Aiken was writing.

There was to be no happy ending to the fairy tale which John Lombe had begun with his daring act of industrial espionage but for reasons which neither he nor his brother could have foreseen.

> *Belfast, July 8.* On Monday last the Corporation of Weavers waited on the Right Hon. and Hon. the

Commissioners of his Majesty's Revenue, with a Memorial under the Corporation Seal, setting forth the great prejudice arising to his Majesty's Revenue, as also to the Silk Manufacture of this Kingdom, by the Importation of French wrought Silk, under English duplicates, which are fraudulently obtained at Chester.

(The Manchester Mercury and Harrop's General Advertiser, 26 July 1763)

After the Seven Years War with France (1756–1763) the illegal bulk importations of superior French silk continued to cause problems, initiating a decline within the English silk industry while the East India Company's activities on the sub-continent were also impacting on the British silk market. Unable to sell their Indian silk products without reducing Indian silk weavers' wages, which were already at a bare minimum, they decided to encourage manufacturers of wrought silk to cease that manufacture and undertake the winding of raw silk. To encourage this object, spinning wheels were smashed and there are stories about maiming workers by the cutting off of thumbs so they could not wind silk. It is unclear whether the East India Company workers or Indian silk workers undertook such barbaric action. There is little in the records to justify this story except William Bolts' description:

Weavers, for daring to sell their goods, and Dallals and Pykars, for having contributed to or connived at such sales, have, by the Company's agents, been frequently seized and imprisoned, confined in irons, fined considerable sums of money, flogged, and deprived, in the most ignominious manner, of what they esteem most valuable, their casts [i.e. they were made to become Dalits]. Weavers also, upon their inability to perform such agreements as have been forced from them by the

Company's agents, have had their goods seized, and sold on the spot, to make good the deficiency: and the winders of raw silk, called *Nagaads*, have been treated also with such injustice, that instances have been known of their cutting off their thumbs, to prevent their being forced to wind silk. This last kind of workmen were pursued with such rigour during Lord Clive's late government in Bengal [1765–1767], from a zeal for increasing the Company's investment of raw silk, that the most sacred laws of society were atrociously violated; for it was a common thing for the Company's seapoys to be sent by force of arms to break open the houses of the Armenian merchants established at Sydabad [i.e. Saidabad, a southern suburb of Murshidabad, the former administrative centre of Bengal] (who have, from time immemorial, been largely concerned in the silk trade) and forcibly take the *Nagaads* from their work, and carry them away to the English factory.

(*Considerations on India Affairs* part 1 p.194, 1772)

The East India Company did not treat their employees well, but they had never done so.

In the provision of the Honourable Company's investment, the rigorous and oppressive measures taken with the manufacturers, in some places, have occasioned *nagaads* or winders of raw silk, to cut off their thumbs, to prevent their being forced to work, though it is better since an increase of pay took place.

In other places weavers have been, by the Company's agents, publicly flogged through their town, and deprived in the most ignominious and cruel manner of what is most valuable to them, their casts, for having only dared to sell in the Bazar a few pieces of cloth of their own manufacturing.

(letter published in *Considerations on India Affairs*, part 2, vol 2, 1775. Appendix F item XXXII)

India is much warmer than Britain, so the woollen, linen and leather clothing generally worn by company employees and their families was hot and uncomfortable. They discovered that Indian weavers produced much lighter materials in the form of fine cottons and muslins. Clothes made from these textiles were colourful, comfortable and cheaper and their popularity grew. Cotton materials were easier to produce and cheaper to buy and were therefore popular, especially with the lower end of the market. Consequently, in India silk began to become more prized as a status symbol and luxury silk goods began to be much in demand.

Derby Silk Mill retained sufficient importance to be included in *The Draper's Dictionary: a manual of textile fabrics: their history and applications.* (Beck, S. William, London. 1882).

Up to this time the silk machinery here was so ineffective that our main supply of organzine was derived from Italy. An attempt made at Derby early in the eighteenth century, by a person named Cotchett, to introduce silk machinery had failed; but more success attended the efforts of John Lombe.

He goes on to re-tell the story of John Lombe and Derby Silk Mill, which was still well-known in 1882, and says that 'this mill was regarded with much wonderment and admiration.'

A contemporary account says of the machinery, that by it – One Hand will Wist as much Silk as before could be done by 50, and that in a truer and better Manner. One

Waterwheel gives Motion to all the rest of the Wheels and Movements, of which any one may be stopped separately. One Fire-Engine likewise conveys warm Air to every individual Part of the Machine, and the whole Work is governed by one Regulator. The House which contains this Engine is of a vast Bulk, and five or six Storeys high.

However, according to Beck in the *Drapers Dictionary*, it was not vengeful Italians who were the main problem faced by the silk mill but 'owlers', smugglers of French silks into England. Mr Beck records that 'The worst evil to which the industry was exposed was the extensive practice of smuggling – a practice so lucrative, in consequence of the high duties, that the "Owlers" as they were called, defied all official vigilance and disregarded all threats of punishment.' Once more he quotes from eighteenth-century officials writing over a century before his own book:

The French writers estimate the average exportation of silks from France to England, during the period from 1688 to 1741, at about 12,500,000 francs a year. In 1763 attempts were made to check the prevalence of smuggling and the silk mercers of the metropolis, to show their anxiety to forward the scheme, are said to have recalled their orders for foreign goods. It would seem, however, either that their patriotic ardour had very soon cooled, or that they had been supplanted by others not quite so scrupulous, for it appears from a report of a committee of the Privy Council, appointed in 1766 to inquire into the subject, that smuggling was then carried on to a greater extent than ever, and that 7,072 looms were out of employment. The same committee reported, that though the French were decidedly superior to us in some branches of the trade, we were quite equal, and even superior to them in others; but instead of proposing, consistently with their report, to admit French silks on a reasonable duty they recommended the continuance of the old system: substituting absolute prohibitions in the place of the prohibitory duties that formerly existed.

Beck then tackled the age-old controversy of adequate wages: a fair day's pay for a fair day's work. In 1773, weavers had succeeded in obtaining legislation for what today might be termed the minimum wage. Beck, however, held this move to be highly detrimental.

Whatever immediate advantages the manufacturers might have reaped from this measure, the ultimate tendency of which could not fail of being most injurious, were effectually countered by the turbulent proceedings of the workmen, who succeeded in obtaining from the Legislature an Act quite sufficient to have destroyed even a prosperous trade. The Spitalfields Act entitled the weavers of Middlesex to demand a fixed price for their labour, which should be settled by the magistrates, while both masters and men were restricted from giving or receiving more or less than the fixed price the manufacturers were liable in heavy penalties if they employed weavers out of the district. The monopoly which the manufacturers had hitherto enjoyed, though incomplete, had had sufficient influence to render inventions and discoveries of comparatively rare occurrence in the silk trade; but the Spitalfields Act extinguished every germ of improvement. It is not, however, to be denied that Macclesfield, Manchester, Norwich, Paisley, &c, are under obligations to this Act; had it extended to the whole kingdom it would have totally destroyed the manufacture, but being confined to Middlesex, it gradually drove the most valuable branches [of the silk industry] from Spitalfields to places where the rate of wages was determined by the competition of the parties, on the principle of mutual interest and compromised advantage.

Still quoting from official reports and emphasising his point, Beck continued:

> As the effects of this Act did not immediately manifest themselves, it was at first exceedingly popular. About 1785, however, the substitution of cottons in the place of silk gave a severe check to the manufacture, and the weavers then began to discover the real nature of the Spitalfields Act. Being forbidden from working at reduced wages, they were totally thrown out of employment so that, in 1793, upwards of 4,000 Spitalfields looms were quite idle. In 1798 the trade began to revive and continued to extend slowly till 1815 and 1816, when the Spitalfields weavers were again involved in sufferings far more extensive and severe than at any former period.
>
> (McCulloch. 1892)

However, Beck does not clarify whether it was the Napoleonic wars and their aftermath, the two years (1815 and 1816) when there was no summer (due to volcanic eruptions in Indonesia) which caused famine through the failure of the harvests, or market forces, which caused their sufferings.

Chapter 13

The Water Frame Controversy and Richard Arkwright

The water frame, a spinning machine powered by water, was said to have been invented by Richard Arkwright in 1768. However, a water frame is simply a spinning frame powered by a waterwheel and these have been known since Antiquity. Richard Arkwright was an entrepreneur with money to invest after his financially advantageous second marriage, and today he would have had a successful career in sales and marketing, but he was not an inventor, nor did he have a particularly mechanical mindset. He took the ideas of others and used them to further his own ambitions. Arkwright chose his workers well and he knew the law, or so he thought, until his desire for fame and fortune finally led him to take matters a step too far.

Lewis Paul

Little is known about Lewis Paul's early life, except that he was 'a foreigner' (Baines, E. *The History of Cotton Manufacture*, 1835), but he was the son of a Huguenot refugee who was physician to Lord Shaftesbury. By the 1730s, Paul had arrived in Birmingham and in 1732 he met John Wyatt, a carpenter working for a gun barrel forger. Consequently, 'by the end of 1733 John Wyatt had built a prototype of a cotton-spinning machine' and together they worked on Paul's idea of inventing a new roller spinning machine with two sets of rollers working at different speeds. Subsequently, 'in 1738 they jointly patented their new invention with the flyer and bobbin system' which was markedly similar to the Italian throwing machine, 'the wire flyer method of twisting yarn was partly the basis for the development of the water frame by Richard Arkwright.' (Calladine, A. *Lombe's Mill*. p.97).

Initially this new machine, which drew cotton and wool through successively faster rollers to give a more even thickness, was powered by a donkey and was used by mills in Birmingham and Northampton. However, the machine proved to be unreliable, so Paul and Wyatt set about improving it and took out a second patent in 1758. In the meantime, in 1748, Paul had also invented a carding machine which was worked by hand, not by animal power or water power. However, in 1759, Lewis Paul died, and subsequently his roller spinning machine was used by Richard Arkwright as part of the model for the water frame; his carding machine model was also used by Arkwright.

Rev. John Dyer of Northampton commemorated the Paul and Wyatt cotton-spinning machine very clearly in a poem of 1757:

> A circular machine, of new design
> In conic shape: it draws and spins a thread
> Without the tedious toil of needless hands.
> A wheel invisible, beneath the floor,
> To ev'ry member of th' harmonius frame,
> Gives necessary motion. One intent
> O'erlooks the work; the carded wool, he says,
> So smoothly lapped around those cylinders,
> Which gently turning, yield it to yon cirque
> Of upright spindles, which with rapid whirl
> Spin out in long extent an even twine.

The Science Museum states that Richard Arkwright's patent no 931, granted on 3 July 1769, used the drawing roller method invented by Lewis Paul in 1738:

> the fibres being teased out by the actions of pairs of rollers running at different speeds and then twisted, as in a spinning wheel, to make a firm yarn. … The motive power comes from a horse mill geared to a vertical shaft with a large pulley which drives the spindles by means of a belt. … The upright shaft of a friction wheel gives motion to the rollers.

However, the detailed descriptions given by Thomas Lombe when applying for patent no 422 in 1718 for the new silk-throwing machinery (p.64–9) show distinct similarities with both Paul's and Arkwright's patents, especially in the use of rollers, and it is clear that the Italian machinery had provided the original blueprint which was then improved upon by Lewis Paul, Thomas Highs and John Kay, just as Italian engineers and inventors had improved upon designs of such machinery since the time of the Crusades and more particularly after the Black Death pandemic of 1347–1349. Leonardo da Vinci, influenced by Martini (who himself had been influenced by Taccola p.27–8) had some of Martini's notebooks in his possession and Leonardo, in turn, had then improved upon the silk-throwing machinery of his day. In addition, Leonardo also invented an automatic bobbin winder. In Italy it seemed to be a natural evolutionary process for engineers of subsequent generations, who had their own ideas, to improve upon the work of those who had gone before them, although they did not derive exclusivity or great riches from their own ingenuity. Arkwright's problem was that he was not an engineer. He took the ideas from others who did the work for him, then patented their work as his own to prevent anyone else improving upon it so he could capitalise on the resulting revenue and was not required to share it with anyone else. Two hundred and fifty years after Arkwright's actions there is still a quirk of English law which states that the copyright for new ideas or inventions discovered through work done in paid employment for others does not belong to the inventing employee but to the employer (section 39 of the Patents Act 1977), and, as in Arkwright's day, this still causes resentment. Whatever the case, Arkwright took his ideas from those who did not work for him, notably the Lombes, Thomas Highs and Lewis Paul.

The German contribution

Water power is greater than human power so the use of water as a power source reduced the labour required and increased the spindle count which produced stronger yarn. In 1760, before Arkwright supposedly started work on the water frame, a German gentleman by the name of Johann Heinrich Bockmöhl (1738–1802) developed a water frame in Elberfeld, Prussia. His father was a bleacher and Johann had followed suit. Dutch and French silk-throwing machinery may have inspired him although this machinery was inferior to the Italian silk-throwing machines. His invention proved easy to use and automatically switched off if a thread broke. Ironically, a German entrepreneur, Johann Gottfried Brügelmann, had also discovered the mechanical secrets of water frames and built them himself and then made use of them by opening a spinning factory at Ratingen in 1783 which he named 'Cromford' after the cotton mill built at Cromford in 1771 by Richard Arkwright. Bockmöhl, however, at least realised that he and Arkwright were both really just entrepreneurs making fortunes from other people, their ideas and hard work.

Richard Arkwright

English schoolchildren learn that Richard Arkwright invented the water frame (1768/9) and James Hargreaves invented the spinning jenny (1764/5) which kick-started a revolution in the manufacture of textiles and consequently inspired the developments of Samuel Crompton's mule (1779), Edmund Cartwright's power loom (1784/5), as well as Eli Whitney's cotton gin (1793/4) which offered yet further refinements. However, this was not the first industrial revolution, just the best known and perhaps the major one. Richard Arkwright has been generally credited as the 'Father of the textile revolution and factory system', although this is a totally false premise.

Richard Arkwright was born in Preston just ten years after the death of John Lombe. His father was a tailor who could not afford to send the young Richard to school. He was taught to read and write by one of his cousins and then apprenticed to a barber in nearby Kirkham. In 1754 he moved to Bolton and, as well as cutting hair, he learned how to make wigs, which were very popular at the time. After his second marriage in 1761, which was financially very advantageous for him, he set up his own barber's shop in Bolton. He was interested in hair dyes and during this time he invented a waterproof dye suitable for periwigs, the fashionable styled wigs worn by both sexes during the eighteenth century. By now he was an accomplished wig maker and consequently he travelled a good deal to obtain the hair and powders necessary to create his wigs. He would have been well aware of the commercial success of the new silk-manufacturing industry and the idea of establishing a dedicated factory like John Lombe's silk mill in Derby would have appealed to him. He would also have been well aware of the East India Company activities and its trade with India, and he would have heard the stories about the fine and colourful Indian cottons which were growing in popularity and which were much more affordable than silk. The East India Company had been importing calicoes, a cheap type of cotton, in increasing quantities since the 1740s. Calicoes were durable, washable and kept their colour. British colonial rule held the Indian sub-continent in a stranglehold so, in order to prevent competition from Indian cottons, Britain imposed restrictive import measures on Indian cottons while at the same time forcing the Indian markets to buy British cotton goods at inflated prices. By the 1760s it would have been obvious to him that new fashions were going to be cotton based, rather than silk based, because they were cheaper and lighter than silk, and, since Britain had ruined the Indian cotton trade, the British held a virtual monopoly over the manufacture of cotton products. Arkwright had always had the air of an entrepreneur and an instinctive knowledge of where there was money to be made, and it became crystal clear to him that the new cottons, rather than the luxury silk industry, would be the way to go for investment opportunities and returns.

Thomas Highs/Hayes

It was at this point that fate intervened. Thomas Highs, or Hayes, (1718–1803) was born in nearby Leigh, just under 8 miles from Bolton, and spent most of his life in the town where he worked as a reed maker. A reed is a strip attached to the batten of a loom which keeps the warp threads well separated so the weft threads can be tightly packed in between these threads. Always keen to improve on means of textile production, Highs had begun to think seriously about designing a spinning machine. Lewis Paul had developed the carding machine and patented his own roller spinning device in 1738, but after he died in 1759 the market remained wide open, so in 1763 Highs employed a close neighbour, John Kay, to help him translate his own ideas into reality.

John Kay

John Kay was born in Warrington, and, although his dates are not certain, he is not to be confused with a contemporary of the same name, John Kay, who invented the flying shuttle in 1733. John Kay from Warrington was a clock-maker by trade who had moved to Leigh and, at some point in 1763, he agreed to work with Thomas Highs on a proposed engine designed to spin thread using rollers. They worked on this project together from 1763–1764/5 until Highs discovered a method of spinning by rollers on very similar principles to those of Lewis Paul. As Lewis Paul was now dead, Highs and Kay set about perfecting their own method of spinning by rollers, at least partly based on the models made from the plans of Lewis Paul. Warrington is only 10 miles from Leigh and Kay had kept in close contact with his family and friends in the town, visiting as often as he could. In 1767, while on one of his periodic visits to Warrington, he met Richard Arkwright, purely by chance, so it is said, in one of the town's public houses. The two men got talking and during their conversation John Kay told Arkwright of the work he had done with Thomas Highs.

The Arkwright/Kay 'Partnership'.

Arkwright was on his travels seeking supplies for his wig-making activities. He was only 22 miles from his Bolton home, but was in no hurry to return. His chance meeting with John Kay proved to be most interesting to Arkwright in terms of potential and he began considering his options. He held more meetings with Kay and six months after meeting Arkwright, John Kay moved back to Warrington and agreed to become Arkwright's 'workman', initially indenturing himself to Arkwright for twenty-one years. At first, Arkwright simply commissioned him to make brass wheels for a 'perpetual motion machine' but subsequently persuaded him to build 'a roller-based spinning machine', based on the work he had done with Thomas Highs, which would later lead to accusations that Kay had stolen Highs' ideas. Fearful that this new project might be discovered and gossiped about by others, Arkwright moved back to Preston in 1768 and took John Kay with him so that they could work secretly on their 'invention'. Gossip in Preston was rife, however, so, in 1769, they both moved to Nottingham to complete their work. Once completed, Arkwright patented the new machine, but he did not tell John Kay. Kay learned of the patent during a chance conversation with James Hargreaves, who had invented the spinning jenny in 1764 and who also lived in Nottingham. Kay was absolutely furious. He told Hargreaves that it was he who had invented the new spinning machine, not Arkwright. This led to a showdown and a huge row between John Kay and Richard Arkwright. Arkwright accused Kay of leaking the secret design of the 'new' machine to Hargreaves and Kay accused Arkwright of stealing his working tools. Arkwright then dismissed Kay's claim to any benefit from the patent by saying that Kay was simply his 'workman' and therefore anything produced during his time with Arkwright was considered Arkwright's property. The row continued with accusations and counter accusations until, in the end, Kay lost his temper completely, storming out of Arkwright's Nottingham house and dissolving their partnership. The legalities of this last action would later be questioned in court.

The new spinning machine was initially horse-powered, but that proved to be cumbersome, and in 1771 Arkwright built a water-powered mill in Cromford which allowed the machinery to be powered by water from the River Derwent. John Lombe's silk mill of 1719 had been powered in the same manner, on the Italian model, but it was Arkwright's mill which was said to be revolutionary, despite the existence in Italy of water-powered mills in preceding centuries and the success of Derby Silk Mill due to water power fifty years beforehand. Arkwright's copying of other people's ideas, machinery and manufactories made him a rich man. However, he left Thomas Highs and John Kay penniless, and his greed for patents and exclusivity, so that others had to pay him for the use of machinery and ideas which were not his, caused great resentment among other manufacturers, and these actions proved to be a very costly mistake.

Chapter 14

The Early Court Cases

In 1781, Arkwright brought a number of court cases against people for 'invading his patent for a complete system of carding and roving for which he had taken out a second patent on 16 December 1775'. This patent contained a number of items 'borrowed' from various spinners. The spinners had, not unnaturally, continued using their own contributions to which Arkwright vociferously objected. In the end he only took proceedings against one person, a gentleman named Colonel Mordaunt, who was brought to trial at the Court of the King's Bench in July 1781. Mordaunt's defence was that 'Mr Arkwright had not fully communicated his inventions on the specification, as required by law, therefore the patent was invalid.' Judge and jury agreed that 'instead of disclosing his inventions in the specification, Arkwright had described them in a confused and unintelligible manner' and consequently Arkwright lost his case.

Soon afterwards Arkwright retaliated by publishing 'The Case' (Richard Arkwright, *A case for the consideration of Parliament, relative to his invention of an Engine for spinning Cotton into Yarn,* printed in 1782) as a vindication of his claims. He began by citing the story of James Hargreaves, who invented the spinning jenny, but had been forced to give up his patent rights by a group of interested parties who collaborated against him so that he could not afford to fight them and he had to relinquish his rights. Arkwright cites the date for the invention of the spinning jenny as 1767, the year that Arkwright and Kay say they first met, but in fact the spinning jenny was invented three years earlier in 1764 when Kay and

Highs had just begun working together. Arkwright then continues putting his 'Case' in the third person singular, as though he were describing someone else, which sounds strange to modern ears but was a concept often employed during the late eighteenth and early nineteenth centuries.

> Mr Arkwright, after many years intense and painful application, invented, about the year 1768, his present method of spinning cotton, but upon very different principles from any invention that had gone before it. He obtained a patent in the year 1769 for making cotton, flax and wool into yarn. But finding that the common method of preparing the materials for spinning was very imperfect, tedious and expensive, he turned his thoughts towards the construction of engines for that purpose; and spent several years of intense study and labour, and, at last produced an invention for carding and preparing the materials, founded in some measure on the principles of his first machine, but his last machines being very complicated, and containing some things materially different in their construction, and some others materially different for their use, from the inventions for which his first patent was obtained, he procured a patent for these also in December 1775.

Arkwright went on to claim that when 'the merits of Mr Arkwright's inventions were fully understood' other manufacturers conspired against him, as they had against James Hargreaves, and complained that they

> began to devise means to rob him of his inventions, and profit by his ingenuity. Every attempt that cunning

could suggest for this purpose was made; by the
seduction of his servants and workmen (whom he had
with great labour taught the business) a knowledge of
his machinery and inventions was fully gained.

(This was republished by the House of Commons in 1829.) Richard
Arkwright seemed to be totally unaware of the irony of his own
hypocrisy. He simply saw conspiracies to deprive him everywhere.
He declared that he believed his summary description at the trial of
1781 had been sufficient; that 'had he been aware of the consequences
of omission, he certainly would have been more circumspect in his
description.'

Richard Guest also states that Arkwright's second wife, Margaret
Biggin, whom he married in 1861, came from Leigh, and that it was
through her that Arkwright had first met Highs. It was his second
marriage that had brought extra financial resources for Arkwright,
who had been struggling to earn a decent living as a wig maker.
After his marriage, he began experimenting with hair dyes for wigs
and invented a waterproof dye which was proving very popular with
his customers. This was some way from inventing cotton-spinning
machinery, but, as his wig business was now thriving and he had
additional financial backing, it made sense that he was looking for
something in which he could invest and make substantial sums of
money.

However, Guest states that, although Arkwright was acquainted
with Highs and his work with spinning inventions, he did not
obtain any knowledge of them from Highs himself. He knew
about John Kay, but, although Kay worked with Highs from
1763 to 1766, Arkwright did not introduce himself to Kay until
the summer of 1767 after Kay and Highs had ceased working
together. Had he approached Thomas Highs for information
about his work, or the project Highs and Kay had worked on

together and been rebuffed? Arkwright also insisted that John Kay himself had suggested that Arkwright should focus his attention on making machines to spin cotton and that Kay offered to make a model of the machine Highs had been working on, which was in fact the water frame or throstle. By 1769 Arkwright had his first patent and, just two years later, in 1771, his own mill at Cromford. The dating sequence tends to suggest some long-term planning on Arkwright's part, not to mention a little of the 'cunning' he ascribed to others because he wanted a patent of machinery which would give him exclusive use and control of that machinery. He knew he was not an inventor; he was an entrepreneur, but a good one with access to resources.

However, the expiry of Arkwright's patents was debated with some enthusiasm.

> Happening to be at Matlock, in the summer of 1784, I fell in company with some gentlemen of Manchester, when the conversation turned on Arkwright's spinning machinery. One of the company observed, that as soon as Arkwright's patent expired, so many mills would be erected, and so much cotton spun, that hands never could be found to weave it. To this observation I replied that Arkwright must then set his wits to work to invent a weaving mill. This brought on a conversation on the subject, in which the Manchester gentlemen unanimously agreed that the thing was impracticable; and in defence of their opinion, they adduced arguments which I certainly was incompetent to answer or even to comprehend, being totally ignorant of the subject, having never at that time seen a person weave. I controverted, however, the impracticability of the thing, by remarking that there

had lately been exhibited in London, an automaton figure, which played at chess. Now you will not assert, gentlemen, said I, that it is more difficult to construct a machine that shall weave, than one which shall make all the variety of moves which are required in that complicated game. (Edmund Cartwright [who invented the power loom])

(Supplement to the *Encyclopædia Britannica* 1801, 1803; and cited by Guest [1823])

The predictions of Edmund Cartwright's companion proved to be true and it is ironic that Cartwright invented the first modern power loom (Leonardo da Vinci had also invented a power loom around 1490) shortly after this conversation at Matlock in 1784. Richard Guest, writing forty years later in 1823, had the benefit of hindsight and was able to record:

In the year 1780, there were twenty Water Frame factories, the property of Mr. Arkwright, or of persons who had paid him a consideration for permission to use his machines. After the repeal of the patent in 1785, the number of factories rapidly increased, and in 1790, there were one hundred and fifty in England and Wales. About 1790, factories were also built for the Jenny; in these factories the cotton was carded and roved by the newly invented machines, which furnished weft better in quality and lower in price, than that spun on the smaller Jennies in the houses of the weavers. Carding, roving and spinning were now given up in the cottages, and the women and children formerly employed in those operations, applied themselves to the Loom. The invention of the Mule, by enabling spinners to make finer yarns than any the

Jenny and Water Frame could produce, gave birth to the muslin manufacture, and found employment for this additional number of weavers.

(Guest, Richard. *A Compendious History of the Cotton-manufacture: With a Disproval of the Claim of Sir Richard Arkwright to the Invention of Its Ingenious Machinery.*

J. Pratt, 1823)

Richard Guest was supported in many of his views by Edward Baines who wrote *History of the Cotton Manufacture in Great Britain* (Fisher, Fisher and Jackson. 1835). Baines, however, had further information and conclusions to offer. He quoted Lewis Paul's patent of June 1738 for the spinning of wool and cotton using rotating pairs of rollers, cylinders or cones, over thirty years before Arkwright took out his patent in 1769, before insisting that Lewis Paul was not the inventor of this system. Baines asserts that Lewis Paul took out the patent in his name, but the real inventor was a man named John Wyatt (1700–1766), a carpenter who lived in Birmingham. Other sources indicate that Wyatt and Paul worked on the invention together, and some that it was Lewis Paul who invented the rollers, but a paper by John Kennedy (1769–1855, a notable Scottish-born cotton-machinery manufacturer in Manchester), published in the Memoirs of the Manchester Literary and Philosophical Society, stated that 'the patent [for spinning by rollers] had always been referred to as Wyatt's invention' although it was Paul who actually registered the patent. Again, this may have been due to costs and form filling as in Thomas Highs' case.

Baines claimed to have a letter from John Wyatt and two hanks of cotton yarn 'spun by the spinning engine ... about the year 1741 ... the movement was at that time, turned by two asses, walking around an axis in a large warehouse, near the well in Upper Priory, in Birmingham.' John Kennedy examined this yarn as well and wrote in his paper '*On the Rise and Progress of the Cotton Trade*' (Manchester Literary and Philosophical Society 1819), 'I think it would not be said that it was spun by a similar machine to that of Mr Arkwright, for the fabric is very different from the early productions of Mr Arkwright, and is, I think, evidently spun by a different machine.'

When Kennedy studied the specification of John Wyatt's invention, as given in Lewis Paul's patent, he stated that 'no doubt was left in his mind that the invention was identical in principle with the machine of Arkwright.'

Wyatt also left a manuscript, written in 1743, entitled *A Systematical Essay on the Business of Spinning* containing details of the 'Birmingham manufactory in 1741–2' and also of a 'Northampton manufactory' which was water powered. Lewis Paul was a superintendent at the Birmingham outlet in 1741. Edward Baines states that, at Northampton, which was powered by a waterwheel, 'the engines consisted of several frames, bearing 250 spindles and bobbins; ... the bobbin revolved upon the spindle ... each was moved by a separate wheel and pinion, containing, the one sixty-four teeth, and the other sixty-five.' Baines then goes on to say:

> It is probable that Wyatt adopted the idea of arranging a number of spindles, with bobbins revolving upon them, in a frame, and of turning the spindles and bobbins by distinct wheels, from the machines for throwing silk, introduced by Sir Thomas Lombe, from Italy, and set up in a large mill at Derby. The introduction of the Italian silk-throwing machinery may have set Wyatt to considering whether other materials, as cotton and wool, might not be spun by a similar apparatus. The rollers, however, find no place in the silk machines.

This offers strong contemporary evidence (although it does appear that rollers did play a part) apart from the legal trials, that the celebrated water frame was a mixture of the silk-throwing machinery and the rollers for spinning powered by water (which gave it its name). Thomas Highs and John Kay simply amalgamated, and perhaps further refined, two existing inventions. Arkwright's main contribution was to patent the combination. Improvements and amendments were made by two of Arkwright's workers, Thomas Highs and James Kay, to the silk-spinning machinery which John Lombe had built, and this formed the basis of the water frame, a machine that Arkwright could not describe or sketch despite being the person who had supposedly invented it. There were five court cases against Arkwright for plagiarism within his own lifetime and he lost them all.

Perhaps the last word should rest with Julius Hare. 'In science its main worth is temporary, as a stepping-stone to something beyond. Even the Principia, as Newton, with characteristic modesty entitled his great work, is truly but the beginning of a natural philosophy, and no more an ultimate work than Watt's steam-engine, or Arkwright's spinning machine.' (J.C. Hare. *Guesses at Truth*. Plumptree 1871.)

Throughout all the claims and counter claims one factor remained constant and it was the rollers which became the common denominator for the story of development in spinning processes development. Leonardo da Vinci had understood the theory of using rollers for stretching and tautening of the threads, drawing plans of what he termed 'rollers for friction' sometime between 1480 and 1500. Although these were not developed in his lifetime (he died in 1519), his drawings clearly show two sets of rollers moving one over the other. Although John Kennedy had believed that rollers were not used in silk spinning, he was wrong. Thomas Lombe's specification clearly indicated that rollers were used in spinning silk.

These rollers may well have provided the inspiration for John Wyatt and Lewis Paul to develop their own rollers for use in spinning cotton thread. People, such as Daniel Defoe and Dr Boswell, were allowed to visit Derby Silk Mill, and, as the city is only about 42 miles (68km), a day's ride on horseback, from Birmingham, where Paul and Wyatt lived, they may well have paid a visit. In any case, Lombe's patent had been widely discussed in detail before parliament refused to renew his patent in 1732.

The invention of the water frame wasn't the only false claim that Richard Arkwright made. He also styled himself 'the Father of the English factory system', because he built the mill at Cromford in 1771, but Thomas and John Lombe had already beaten him to it with the building of Derby Silk Mill fifty years beforehand. Arkwright's factory method was copied from the Lombes' silk mill model, and the pattern of building mills five storeys high had persisted since the Lombes' time. However, the first known European factory had been built in Bologna to manufacture silk in the fourteenth century (see p.18).

The modern factory system really marked the end of the cottage industry and the 'putting-out' system; replacing 'hand-made' with 'machinery-made'. All processes were placed in a large building under one roof with common power sources; a kind of 'one stop shop'. The factory system was open to abuse by employers and the rights of workers were not considered in the eighteenth century. They simply existed to serve their masters. Contamination of the air the workers breathed with textile detritus, the heat, the cold, the noise, were all problems which affected workers' health. Lung and digestive issues were common and the continuous working of numerous machines to which workers were exposed for sixty hours a week rendered many completely deaf. No more than ten minutes exposure to such noise levels is currently permitted in 2021. Today the 'factory system' is seen as cruel and repressive because it led to long hours, low wages, poor working conditions and poor living conditions with inadequate ventilation, space, housing and sanitation facilities; as well as the introduction of child labour.

Children from the age of 5 were employed for just a few pence in wages per week and were frequently ill-treated by the factory overseers. Moving from agricultural work to factory work was a huge cultural shock for most workers. On the farms, the cows never minded if they were milked at 5 a.m., 5.30 a.m., 6 a.m., or 6.30 a.m. as long as they were milked. In the towns and cities, workers had to queue up punctually to get work in the factory for the day. The factory gates were opened at 6 a.m. sharp. Punctuality, timescales and deadlines were everything and those arriving at 6.01 a.m. could find the gates slammed in their faces. The so-called 'British obsession' with the clock stems from this time. The mills have long gone but the mindset has not.

In 1781, Arkwright applied to the courts 'to protect his patent rights against infringers'. His case was published in 1782.

> Richard Arkwright, *A case for the consideration of Parliament, relative to his invention of an Engine for spinning Cotton into Yarn*, printed in 1782. Republished in: House of Commons (1829) Report from the Select Committee on the Law Relative to Patents for Inventions.
>
> Mr. Richard Arkwright, after many years study, brought his spinning machinery to bear about 1768: he was a native of Lancashire; but fearing the same fate as Hargrave [*sic*], went to Nottingham, and obtained a patent, dated 3 July 1769, for a machinery for making web or yarn of cotton, flax, or wool. He afterwards found it necessary to apply the same principles to the preparation, and took another patent, dated 16 December 1775, for certain machines for preparing silk, cotton, flax and wool for spinning. During five years after the date of his first patent, Mr. Arkwright and his partners expended £12,000 in machinery and buildings before

any profit was made. The last invention was a very important addition to the first; and by combining them, excellent yarn, or twist, was at last produced; but there was still much difficulty in establishing a trade; for the cotton manufacturers would not have the new yarn at any price, and the proprietors were obliged to weave the yarn, into stockings, and into calicoes; but the latter was restricted by the Excise, which rendered relief by an Act of Parliament necessary.

The manufacture of yarn being at length full established, the demand for it became too great for the patentees to supply, and then they sold licenses very extensively, so that at least £60,000 has been expended in consequence of such grants. Mr. Arkwright and his partners have expended upwards of £30,000 in buildings and machinery in Derbyshire, and above £4,000 in Manchester; and they have lost not less than £5,000 or £6,000 by injuries from mobs, and from fire. The saving of labour by this machinery is several hundred thousand per annum, and yet trade is so greatly increased, that many more people are employed, and can earn a comfortable maintenance, than were employed before. The same inventions may be applied with equal advantage to prepare and spin wool.

To prevent his inventions getting abroad to foreigners, Mr. Arkwright purposely omitted to give so full and particular a description of his inventions, in the specification of his last patent, as he would otherwise have done, believing, from the concluding clause in the patent, that he need not so fully describe. His patent right being largely infringed, he was obliged to prosecute some infringers, although an association was formed to resist him; but on a trial in the King's Bench in July

1781 a verdict was given against him, on the ground that his specification was not as full and accurate as the law requires. Having established a business that already employs above 5,000 persons, and a capital of not less than £200,000, he hopes to be relieved by Parliament, from the consequences of an unintentional error.

This was a step too far and proved too much for Highs and Kay.

Chapter 15

The Final Case against Richard Arkwright

As a result of Highs' and Kay's persistence, the fifth and final case against Richard Arkwright began on 25 June 1785. Thomas Highs, John Kay and his wife, Sarah, would all testify that Richard Arkwright had stolen Thomas Highs' original invention 'by the medium of Mr Kay'. However, Richard Arkwright was not without his supporters.

> The difficulties which Arkwright encountered in organising his factory system, were much greater than is commonly imagined. In the first place, he had to train his work-people to a precision in assiduity altogether unknown before, against which their listless and restive habits rose in continual rebellion; in the second place, he had to form a body of accurate mechanics, very different from the rude hands which then satisfied the manufacturer; in the third, he had to seek a market for his yarns; and in the fourth, he had to resist competition in its most odious forms. From the concurrence of these circumstances, we find that so late as the year 1779, ten years after the date of his first patent, his enterprise was regarded by many as a doubtful novelty.
>
> (Ure, Andrew. *The Cotton Manufacture of Great Britain,* Volume 1. 1836)

Dr Andrew Ure (1778–1837) was a distinguished chemist with conservative views. He wrote with concise detail and gave informed analyses, but he had to rely on other people's assessment of the workers because he was only a baby in 1779 and, by the time of the trial in 1785, he would still have been wearing dresses as was then the custom for young boys.

Ralph Mather painted a rather different picture in his book *An Impartial Representation of the Case of the Poor Cotton Spinners in Lancashire* (1780):

> Arkwright's machines require so few hands, and those only children, with the assistance of an overlooker. A child can produce as much as would, and did upon an average, employ ten grown up persons. Jennies for spinning with one hundred or two hundred spindles, or more, going all at once, and requiring but one person to manage them. Within the space of ten years, from being a poor man worth £5, Richard Arkwright has purchased an estate of £20,000; while thousands of women, when they can get work, must make a long day to card, spin, and reel 5,040 yards of cotton, and for this they have four-pence or five-pence and no more.

The transcripts of the trial of Richard Arkwright in 1785 are repeated courtesy of Richard Guest's transcriptions. They are covered comprehensively and authoritatively in his publication, *A Compendious History of the Cotton-manufacture: with a Disproval of the Claim of Sir Richard Arkwright to the Invention of Its Ingenious Machinery* (J. Pratt, 1823). Guest lays out the trial text for both the prosecution and the defence, practically word for word, which is important because of the nature of the case and its outcome for posterity.

Richard Arkwright preferred to talk about himself in the third person when discussing formal matters in the same way the Duke of Wellington would address parliament when opposing electoral reform in the early nineteenth century. Arkwright put his case at length and in the third person, as was his wont.

> Mr. Arkwright, after many years intense and painful application, invented, about the year 1768, his present method of spinning cotton, but upon very different principles from any invention that had gone before it. He was himself a native of Lancashire; but having so recently witnessed the ungenerous treatment of poor Hargrave [*sic*], by the people of that county, he retired to Nottingham, and obtained a patent in the year 1769, for making cotton, flax, and wool into yarn. But, after some experience, finding that the common method of preparing the materials for spinning (which is essentially necessary to the perfection of good yarn) was very imperfect, tedious, and expensive, he turned his thoughts towards the construction of engines for that purpose; and, in the pursuit, spent several years of intense study and labour, and at last produced an invention for carding and preparing the materials, founded in some measure on the principles of his first machine. These inventions, united, completed his great original plan. But his last machines being very complicated, and containing some things materially different in their construction, and some others materially different in their use, from the inventions for which his first patent was obtained, be procured a patent for these also in December, 1775.
>
> (Guest, Richard, 1823)

Arkwright appeared to be haunted by the case of James Hargrave [*sic*] who invented the spinning jenny only to have his initial invention destroyed, his eventual patent right 'invaded' and taken from him, because he could not afford to fight for it in the courts, then dying 'in obscurity and great distress'.

However, this did not stop Arkwright from repeating history, and he continued to put his case forcefully, oblivious to the fact that he was doing to Highs and Kay exactly what had been done to James Hargreaves, and that which Arkwright feared so much might happen in his own case.

> No sooner were the merits of Mr. Arkwright's inventions fully understood, from the great increase of materials produced in a given time, and the superior quality of the goods manufactured; no sooner was it known, that his assiduity and great mechanical abilities were rewarded with success; than the very men, who had before treated him with contempt and derision, began to devise means to rob him of his inventions, and profit by his ingenuity. Every attempt that cunning could suggest for this purpose was made; by the seduction of his servants and workmen, (whom he had with great labour taught the business) a knowledge of his machinery and inventions was fully gained. From that time many persons began to pilfer something from him; and then by adding something else of their own, and by calling similar productions and machines by other names, they hoped to screen themselves from punishment. So many of these artful and designing individuals had at length infringed on his patent right, that he found it necessary to prosecute several: but it was not without great difficulty, and considerable expence [*sic*], that he was able to make any proof against them; conscious that

their conduct was unjustifiable, their proceedings were conducted with the utmost caution and secrecy. Many of the persons employed by them were sworn to secrecy, and their buildings and workshops were kept locked up, or otherwise secured. This necessary proceeding of Mr. Arkwright, occasioned, as in the case of poor Hargrave [*sic*], an association against him, of the very persons whom he had served and obliged. Formidable, however, as it was, Mr. Arkwright persevered, trusting that he should obtain in the event, that satisfaction which he appeared to be justly entitled to.

Richard Arkwright appeared not to notice any possible hypocrisy or irony as he pursued his theme.

A trial in Westminster Hall, in July last, at a large expence [*sic*], was the consequence; when, solely by not describing so fully and accurately the nature of his last complex machines as was strictly by law required, a verdict was found against him. Had he been at all aware of the consequences of such omission, he certainly would have been more careful and circumspect in his description. It cannot be supposed that he meant a fraud on his country: it is on the contrary, most evident that he was anxiously desirous of preserving to his native country the full benefit of his inventions. Yet he cannot but lament, that the advantages resulting from his own exertion and abilities alone, should be wrested from him by those who have no pretension to merit; that they should be permitted to rob him of his inventions before the expiration of the reasonable period of fourteen years, merely because he has unfortunately omitted to point out all the minutiae of his complicated machines. In short, Mr. Arkwright has chosen a subject in manufactures (that of spinning) of all others the most general, the most interesting, and the most difficult. He has, after near twenty years unparalleled diligence and application, by the force of natural genius, and an unbounded invention, (excellencies seldom united) brought to perfection machines on principles as new in theory, as they are regular and perfect in practice. He has induced men of property to engage with him to a large amount; from his important inventions united, he has produced better goods, of their different kinds, than were ever before produced in this country; and finally, he has established a business that already employs upwards of five thousand persons, and a capital, on the whole, of not less than £200,000, a business of the utmost importance and benefit to this kingdom.

The transcripts of the trial, both for the prosecution and defence, are rather wordy but essential because of the importance of the conclusions they verify, which was that Arkwright did not invent the water frame. Legal procedures and lines of questioning witnesses have not changed much and Serjeant Bolton who examined Thomas Highs in the witness box was extremely thorough. Once he had established the identity and trade of Mr Highs he got down to business.

SB. Have you been employed to make machines for manufacturers?

TH. I have.

SB. Look at this carding machine, with the two cylinders, the great one and the little one – how long ago have you seen one of those?

TH. It is about twelve years; between twelve and thirteen years.

SB. Was your little cylinder like that, covered over with needles?

TH. Covered over with cards, it was.

SB. Do you happen to remember telling Mr Arkwright about this?

TH. About this, Sir?

SB. Aye!

TH. No, not about that.

SB. But about the machine that was made?

TH. No, I did not tell him about that, it was made after I had some discourse with Mr Arkwright.

SB. When was it you had that discourse with Arkwright?

TH. It might be about thirteen years since – I cannot just remember everything.

SB. I will take you [now] to the rollers. Look at the rollers through which the thread comes, the roving or spinning, or whatever it is called. Did you ever see rollers like those before 1775, before Mr Arkwright's patent?

TH. I have seen rollers. I made rollers myself in 1767.

SB. You made rollers yourself in 1767?

TH. Yes, Sir.

SB. Have you looked at them? You see one is fluted, the other is covered with leather?

TH. I see it is.

SB. Was yours the same way?

TH. Yes, mine was, two years after, but not then.

SB. Not at first?

TH. No.

SB. In 1769 yours were like it?

TH. They were, mine had fluted work; fluted wood, upon an iron axis; but the other roller was the same, only it was covered with shoe leather, instead of that leather.

SB. Who did you employ when you first conceived this invention; who did you employ to make it for you?

TH. I employed one Kay, who came from Warrington.

SB. What trade was he?

TH. He followed clock-making, at that time.

SB. You employed him to make it?

TH. Yes I employed him to make a small model, with four wheels, of wood, to show him the method it was to work in, and desired him at the same time to make me brass wheels, that would multiply it about five to one.

SB. Look at that and see whether it is upon the same principle?

TH. No, not exactly so; the wheels were not exactly so.

SB. Who made you the wheels?

TH. I made them myself.

SB. Describe what you mean by multiplying five to one?

TH. By making the different rollers go, one faster than the other.

SB. Was that for the purpose of drawing the thread finer?

TH. Yes Sir.

At this point, Mr Erskine, another member of the legal team, pointed out to the judge that he should note that 'the only description given by Mr Arkwright, for his rollers, falls in directly with this man's description.'

SB. Do you remember being at Manchester Races [in] 1767?

TH. No.

SB. Did you see Mr Arkwright at any time?

TH. I suppose about twenty years – or twenty-one years since.

Arkwright had tried to claim that he and Highs had not met until 1767 but Highs put the date as 1764/1765. There was a subsequent meeting between the two men around 1772 at which Highs told Arkwright that he knew Arkwright had hired Kay after Highs and Kay had worked together and that but for Highs' contribution Kay and Arkwright 'would never have had the rollers'.

SB. What discourse had you with Arkwright about the rollers?

TH. I told him he would never have known them but for me; and he put his hand in this manner – to his knee and that was the answer he gave – also he told me, when I told him it was my invention, suppose it was, he says, if it was, he says, if any man has found out a thing, and begun a thing and does not go forwards, he lays it aside, and any other man has a right in so many weeks or months – another man has a right to take it up and get a patent for it.

NB Applying for and obtaining patents in the eighteenth century was a complicated and expensive business and Highs would have been too poor to be able to do so.

SB. Have you actually made, or not, any of these carding machines?

TH. I have made carding machines, but not with these individual things, as this is; there are various forms.

SB. Did you ever make a machine that gives a perpetual roving?

TH. Yes, I did, the very same as that is.

SB. That it made a continual roving?

TH. Yes.

SB. Had you a little cylinder, like that, to take off the cotton from the large one?

TH. I had a cylinder, like that, to take off the cotton from the large one – [but] both my cylinders were of a size.

SB. But, however, that cylinder behind took off from the other cylinder, for perpetual carding?

TH. Yes, Sir.

Before cross-examination Highs stated that he had made four or five similar machines and had sold them to manufacturers during the early 1770s, but that he had only made one of the type shown to the court. Serjeant Adair then began his cross-examination.

SA. You never made but one in that method?

TH. No.

Highs said he had made this single machine around 1772 but it had not really done the work for which the customer had ordered it.

SA. What was the nature of that?

TH. To take the carding off perpetually.

SA. What sort of carding?

TH. Just such as is round this, only garters were put on in the same way; first and foremost, I made a cylinder of a board, and got it turned, I had workmen of my own: then when that was turned, I had got a mahogany board, and made them the breadth of the card, to fit; after that, when I had screwed them on with screws upon that cylinder, I drew them over that cylinder; then I got them throwed again, or turned; and after that I took and dressed the edges of the card a little narrower, to give liberty for the other to come in; I took the card this way and laid it down sideways, to take up but little room, and by that means it brought the teeth so close together, as made a perpetual carding.

Having repeated some of this information and asked where the machine had been used, Serjeant Adair resumed his cross-examination.

124

SA. What use did you put these rollers to, that were in proportion five to one?

TH. I made them on purpose to spin cotton.

SA. To spin?

TH. Yes and to rove too.

SA. Upon your oath, did you ever apply them to roving of cotton.

TH. I will tell you how I did it: I got a board of flat wood, as this is; I took the carding first, and rolled it with another board, til it was a little harder; I laid the card loose at first; then I run it through the roller, to make it stronger; then I put them all together through and through again, til we made it coarse thread as this is; afterwards I put in the coarse thread, I put it in the roller again, and made it fine.

At this point, it was clarified to the court that roving and spinning were done with the same rollers. Serjeant Adair then asked Highs when and where he intended to apply these rollers for use.

TH. In the town of Leigh – I was only improving myself – I had a large family at that time and was not able to follow it. I thought, when I became a little abler, I could get a friend to assist me, being poor – I was not willing anybody should steal it from me.

SA. Now, Mr Highs, this was an experiment you made for your information?

TH. Undoubtedly; I used but two spindles at that time.

SA. You meant to preserve the benefit of it, if afterwards you should be able to avail yourself of it?

TH. I did, Sir.

SA. Now what knowledge had you, how came you to suppose, Mr Arkwright got that from you?

TH. I have no further knowledge than [John] Kay's wife told me.

SA, You, yourself don't know?

TH. I cannot tell which way he got it.

Some discussion followed in the court as to the technicalities of the machinery and its working mode which was then summed up by Mr Erksine.

'My Lord; we say; this difference of wheels, invented by this most ingenious man [Highs], was taken by Mr Arkwright from him, and he claims the whole benefit of it by this patent, and we say, that destroys the whole of his patent.'

The next person to take the stand was John Kay, the vital link between Thomas Highs' work and Richard Arkwright. He was examined by Mr Lee who established that Kay met Arkwright in Warrington in 1767 while the Manchester Races were taking place. They had met casually by chance in a Warrington public house and got talking. There was some suggestion that Arkwright may have known who John Kay was and had approached him for that reason. However, Arkwright said that he wanted 'some bits of brass turned' and Kay had agreed to do them. Arkwright turned up at Kay's house, where he worked, four days in a row with various bits of work for which he paid immediately. After four days, Arkwright asked Kay to join him for a glass of wine to discuss business and asked Kay if his own business was profitable. John Kay then described to the court what happened next.

JK. He asked me what I could get a week. I told him about fourteen shillings: 'Oh', says he, 'I can get more than you', I said 'what business may you be of?'

He said, 'I was a barber, but I have left it off, and I and another are going up and down the country buying hair and can make more of it.'

We were talking of different things, and this thing came up, of spinning by rollers. He said, 'That will never be brought to bear, several gentlemen have almost broke themselves by it.'

I said, 'I think I could bring that to bear'. That was all that passed that night.

The next morning, he comes to my bedside, and says, 'Do you remember what I told you last night?' and asked, could I make him a small model, at a small expense?

'Yes,' says I, 'I believe I can.'

Says he, 'If you will, I will pay you.'

I went and bought a few articles, and made a small wooden model, and he took it with him to Manchester, and in a week or a fortnight's time, I cannot say which, he comes back again, and I made him another.

ML. Before you go further, who did you get the method of making these models from?

JK. From Mr Highs, the last witness.

ML. Did you tell Mr Arkwright so?

JK. I told him, I and another man had tried that at Warrington.

ML. You made him a model?

JK. I made him two models, and he took one to Preston; Burgoyne's election was about that time.

ML. I understand that [the election of General John Burgoyne to the Preston No. 1 seat in the general election] was in 1768 – look at that, [points to model in court] was that the sort of model or was it all like that?

JK. It was with rollers.

ML. It was with double rollers in that way?

JK. Yes, with four pairs of rollers; this has only two.

ML. Were they fluted?

JK. No.

ML. Neither of them?

JK. No.

ML. Neither top nor bottom?

JK. No.

ML. Did they turn equally when at work, or one faster than the other?

JK. No. One faster than the other.

ML. What was the purpose of that?

JK. Why, on purpose to draw cotton out finer.

ML. Where do you live, Kay?

JK. I live at Warrington.

ML. You have seen those kind of things worked?

JK. Yes.

ML. Was the purpose of your discovery, you had from Highs, to do the like things now in that engine?

JK. Yes.

ML. First to rove it, then to make it finer, but to give it a proper consistency?

JK. Yes, we had it roved by a second, a hand wheel at that time.

ML. It was for the purpose of roving, with one roller, and afterwards spinning with the other rollers?

JK. Yes.

ML. After he took your model away, and carried it to Manchester, you had some other conversation with him, do you recollect?

JK. Yes, and I went with him.

ML. Did you live with him there?

JK. I was with him at the time of the election in 1768; about thirteen weeks with him.

ML. Was you working with him as a mechanic?

JK. Yes, I went there to make a clock for him

ML. Now pray did you ever make any other models for him, or for anybody else?

JK. No, not at that time, not till such time as I went to work for him at Nottingham.

ML. You did go afterwards to Nottingham?

JK. Yes.

ML. When?

JK. As soon as the election was over.

ML. That was in March, 1768?

JK. It was ended in April, I believe.

ML. Now, how long did you work with him?

JK. I cannot tell, four or five years perhaps, I cannot say how long.

ML. Well, afterwards Mr Arkwright obtained his patent a considerable distance of time?

JK. Yes.

ML. When did you hear he had obtained it?

JK. James Hargrave [*sic*] came and told me he had got his patent.

ML. Where is he?

JK. He is dead. I could not help myself, you see I did not know anything about it at all.

ML. You must know, whether at that time, it was his own invention, or he had it of you?

JK. James Hargrave [*sic*] told me I should have lodged a caveat.

ML. Don't tell me what James Hargrave said, you must know whether it was his own invention?

JK. I know very well he did not invent the rollers.

ML. You know very well he did not invent the rollers.

JK. No.

ML. On the contrary, you know he had them from you?

JK. Yes.

ML. And you had them from this poor Highs?

JK. Yes.

ML. And you told him so.

JK. I told him so many a time.

Mr Cowper was the cross-examining counsel and he now began to question John Kay.

MC. You lived with him before he gained his patent?

JK. Yes.

MC. Parted with him on good terms?

JK. I don't know upon what terms I parted with him.

MC. Did you leave his home without his knowledge?

JK. Yes.

MC. You fled from his service?

JK. Yes.

MC. By what apprehension did you leave him – was there not a charge of felony against you?

JK. They pretended so, but they could not find anything against me.

MC. I ask, whether you did not fly from him upon the charge of felony?

Objections were raised at this point and Mr Cowper was told to ask Kay who stole the invention to which Cowper hotly retorted, 'there is a deal of difference between stealing a tankard, when invented, or the invention of making a tankard.' He turned back to John Kay.

MC. There was a charge against you, well or ill founded?

JK. I was at Nottingham and he took my property away.

At this point, the judge, Mr Justice Buller, asked who had taken Kay's property.

JK. Mr Arkwright had.

MC. He had taken your goods, had he?

JK. Yes.

MC. Had not you run away from his service upon a charge of felony being exhibited against you?

JK. I cannot tell what was charged against me.

MC. You cannot tell whether you run away upon the fear of a charge?

JK. He told me something when I came back; I did run away.

MC. You heard soon after, of this patent, which you knew to be yours or Highs' invention and not Arkwright's?

JK. Yes.

MC. And you talked of a partnership, I suppose?

JK. Yes.

MC. You made no secret of it?

JK. No.

MC. You being a poor man, it put you to no expense to complain to anybody about the theft of the invention?

JK. No.

MC. Did you apply to anybody when the nine causes were here?

JK. Yes.

MC. Did you hear them talked of, before they were tried, that they were to be so?

JK. Yes.

MC. And did you, before that, publicly complain Arkwright stole those rollers?

JK. Yes.

MC. Were you brought up then?

JK. Yes, Sir.

MC. You was not examined upon the first trial?

JK. No.

MC. Was you examined upon the second trial?

Kay did not answer this question and Mr Lee said that Kay had been put down as a witness. At this point, the judge, Mr Justice Buller, intervened again.

JB. Kay. What were the things Mr Arkwright had taken out of your house?

JK. Several tools.

JB. Were they tools respecting this business?

JK. Yes.

JB. Was that the subject of the charge against you?

JK. Why I was making another machine in my house, to spin jersey, which I thought of while I was at Nottingham, I might compleat [*sic*] it, I believe he thought I was making this machine, and that was his intent.

JB. You was making a spinning machine?

JK. I was making a thing to spin jersey; before I went to Nottingham I pulled that thing to pieces.

JB. You don't understand my question. Were the tools, which Mr Arkwright had taken out of your house, the subject of the charge of felony against you; was it upon that account, he said you was to be charged with felony?

JK. I believe he did; he told my wife I had stole things from him.

JB. Did he take those things, as the things stolen?

JK. No; I brought them out of Lancashire.

JB. Tell what it was Mr Arkwright took away?

JK. Several tools, compasses, pliers, and vice, and other things.

JB. Did he take anything besides tools?

JK. Yes, a pair of sleeves, a spying glass I had, and locks and brass wheels I had brought with me, to make a movement with, from Lancashire; I had not time to make it, and I brought them with me.

JB. What was the spying glass?

JK. That was a small spying glass, which drew into four joints, that was mine, I brought it from Nottingham.

At this point, Mr Erskine interrupted to say that he now had a brief in his hand which showed why John Kay was not called at the trial of 1781. Mr Justice Buller responded to an objection and refused to hear it. Mr Lee then turned to John Kay.

ML. Did Arkwright ever pretend to prosecute you for this pretended felony?

JK. Yes, he offered to do it.

ML. Did he do it?

JK. No, I never saw it.

Mr Justice Buller tried once more.

JB. When did you get back to Nottingham again?

JK. I never went to Nottingham again.

Mr Lee, seeing this was going nowhere, resumed his line of questioning.

ML. It is suggested to me; did Mr Arkwright require you to enter into any obligation or bond, not to do anything in this way of business?

JK. Yes, at the time I was at Preston with him.

ML. In the year 1768?

JK. Yes.

ML. After you had given him that model?

JK. Yes.

ML. Was he then well to live, or in a situation not much better than you were?

JK. He was a poor working man.

ML. He was?

JK. He was, and I too; he got assistance to join him in this affair and I agreed to work for him as a servant.

ML. He got a bond, did he?

JK. Yes.

ML. What was it for?

JK. To serve him for so many years.

At this point, the examination ended – which must have been to the relief of all concerned. John Kay was not an easy man to interrogate, not because he was simple minded or stupid, quite the reverse, but because he did not wish to incriminate himself in any way. Kay was intelligent enough to know that Arkwright had done to Kay what Kay had done to Thomas Highs and that because of Arkwright's action, Kay had left Arkwright's house and employment in a massive huff. John Kay must also have known that Arkwright was not a poor man like Kay himself and he also almost certainly knew that Arkwright had financial backers and business partners. Also, because he was a member of Arkwright's staff, Kay had no automatic rights to be considered in the patent even though he had done much of the inventive work. There have been cases in recent history where an employee working on some project has made a significant breakthrough or contribution but is not entitled to any of the reflected glory because, as an employee, anything researched, discovered or made for their employer during the paid hours of their employment is the property of their employer. It may not be fair but it is how the law operates. By the same principle, Thomas Highs was entitled to the work Kay did for him during the time Highs employed him.

To try and support Kay's case further, Mr Erskine brought Sarah Kay, John Kay's wife, to the witness stand. At this time women had few, if any, rights and could not testify against their husbands, so it was clear that all she could really do was support her husband. However, she could be useful in the verification of certain details. Mr Erskine established that John and Sarah Kay had been married for over twenty-five years and that therefore she could recall events concerning her husband back to the time he first met Highs.

> ME. You remember, then, I suppose, when he [John Kay] worked for Highs?
>
> SK. Yes, I remember his making a small model.
>
> ME. When did you see or know anything about rollers, by which cotton is spun?
>
> SK. That was about the beginning of the year 1763.
>
> ME. Where did you first see it?
>
> SK. At a place called Leigh.
>
> ME. Who had them?
>
> SK. Mr Highs had them.
>
> ME. Do you remember your husband getting any models made of those?
>
> SK. That one I remember, and the one he made for Arkwright. He made one for Highs, and then he made one for Mr Arkwright.

ME. Do you remember when he made the model for Highs?

SK. In the year 1763.

ME. Do you remember when he made the model for Arkwright?

SK. At the time of Bourgoyne's election.

ME. How do you know it was for Arkwright that he made the model?

SK. My husband told me so.

ME. You have seen him and Arkwright together?

SK. Yes, all the day over.

ME. About the time he was getting this model made?

SK. Yes.

ME. And had he this model at the time, to take with him?

SK. Yes, he asked whether he would make him a small model at a small expense.

ME. You saw them together all day?

SK. Yes, after he had made the first model, he took it off with him somewhere or other, and came back to my husband, and asked if he could make another.

ME. He took it off with him somewhere or other, and came back to your husband, and asked if he could make another.

SK. Yes.

ME. Was there another made?

SK. Yes.

ME. Did you see this model of the rollers for drawing the cotton thread?

SK. Yes, for spinning.

Sarah Kay was then briefly cross-examined by Mr Chambre.

MC. You are sure it was in 1763?

SK. In 1763, my husband and Mr Highs began it.

Mr Erskine interjected here.

ME. When was the first model you ever saw?

SK. That my husband made for Mr Highs?

ME. When was that?

SK. In the year 1763.

MC. Now, when was it he made the model for Arkwright?

SK. In the year 1767.

It was becoming painfully clear that the truth was that Richard Arkwright had not invented this machinery himself. Arkwright might well have expected to be believed over his workers because the system favoured employers and workers were expected to be respectful and accommodating to their 'betters'; but although the class system was rife and money was almost everything, the jury found against Arkwright when they discovered that he could not even sketch the machinery he claimed to have spent so long designing and developing. Although John Kay was heavily criticised for breaking his agreement partnership with Richard Arkwright, the case was upheld. The charge was of plagiarism and the evidence of Highs and the Kays, coupled with Arkwright's inability to draw his own invention, indicated that he was guilty as charged and had no right to the patent for something that was not his own work. Of course, those with vested interests were pleased since the refusal to issue a patent to Richard Arkwright meant that other manufacturers were freely able to use his new machinery.

It may have been Arkwright's love of self-promotion which finally led him to overplay his hand. Lewis Paul had invented a carding machine in 1738, and had patented it in 1748, but Arkwright sought a second patent on the carding machine, after a few tweaks to improve its performance. Paul had died in 1759 which left Arkwright with few scruples about using his work. However, that patent too was refused after the Highs Kay case verdict.

At the final trial in 1785, the ten articles contained on Arkwright's specification were again examined carefully and found wanting.

- No. 1. A hammer worked by a cog wheel was proved to have been described and engraved in Emmerson's Mechanics in 1773.
- No. 2. The examining witnesses could not tell what this was used for until one of them stated he believed it was first used for beating hemp by workers in Mr Arkwright's factory but other workers deposed that they had never seen it.
- No. 3. The feeder of the carding engine had been used by Henry Marsland in 1771 and that Arkwright saw it when he had paid a call to Marsland's works and had it copied. John Lees also proved that he had invented a similar feeder in 1772.
- No. 4. The crank was proved to have been invented by James Hargreaves in 1772 by Hargeaves, his wife, son and colleagues.

- No. 5. Filleted cards on the second roller nailed around the cylinder in circular fashion were proved by Mr Pilkington to have been invented by Mr Wood in 1774.
- No. 6. Two pairs of rollers, one revolving faster than the other, were proved by Thomas Highs, John and Sarah Kay, to have been invented by Thomas Highs at Leigh in 1767.
- No. 7. The roving can which Benjamin Butler proved was used in 1759, and which Betty Kennion and Joseph Woolley roved, were used in Binyon's factory in 1773/1774.
- No. 8. The witnesses had no idea what this was used for, and Arkwright's counsel admitted that it was not used for preparing cotton nor for spinning.
- No. 9. The spindle used by Thomas Highs for the water frame in 1767 and previously used in the flax or treadle wheel.
- No. 10. None of the witnesses could describe the use of this shaft or spindle which was on a pulley or drum.

It was proved, therefore, that all the component parts of Arkwright's machines were 'borrowed' from other inventors, and it was suggested that Arkwright had wanted his specification to be as obscure and enigmatic as possible so that other people could not copy or make the components when the patent expired. Mr W.D. Croft, who was employed by Arkwright to draw up the specification, said as much in the witness box when he admitted that Mr Arkwright had told him 'he wished it to act as a specification, but to be as obscure as the nature of the case would possibly admit.' Arkwright had used his wealth to piece together an 'invention' composed entirely of other people's work and intended to reap rich rewards from the work of others. Neither judge, judiciary nor jury were fooled and one of the jurors simplified the reason for turning down Arkwright's claim for a patent. 'He said he spent all this time inventing this machine, but he couldn't even sketch it.'

Chapter 16

Aftermath of the Court Cases

Despite losing his court cases for plagiarism, Richard Arkwright died a rich and respected man with a knighthood while Thomas Highs returned to reed making and died almost unknown in near poverty.

In 1786, the year after this last court case, Richard Arkwright received his knighthood. He was now able to move in more exalted circles and evidence suggests he may have been quite an adept social climber. It is difficult to judge a personality when they have been dead for 230 years, but actions can speak much louder than words, so people judge others, like for example, Napoleon or Hitler or Lucretia Borgia, on what they did rather than who they were. When Sir Richard Arkwright died in 1792, he left a fortune of £500,000, worth over £55 million at today's values. Yet for Highs and Kay, who had helped him to make his fame and fortune, there was nothing. There never would be anything. Thomas Highs died in poverty. John Kay earned a pittance as his 'workman' but Kay had believed he was in partnership with Arkwright and would see some return when their machinery began to sell. Once he had left Arkwright's employ, he never saw another penny from Arkwright, and he too died impoverished. However, Arkwright's dealings with Georgiana, Duchess of Devonshire, with whom he had become friends, were quite different. Unlike Highs and Kay, she had the total respect of Arkwright because she was married to the fifth Duke of Devonshire, one of the richest and most powerful dukes in the country. Chatsworth, the Devonshire family seat, is only 10 miles from Cromford where Richard Arkwright had made his home.

It was almost inevitable that they would meet at some point and Arkwright considered it a great honour to know her. The Duchess was a high society beauty who was extremely 'fashionable' and intelligent. She was deeply involved with the Whigs politically and a kind of 'influencer' of her day, but she had what would turn out to be, for her, a ruinous problem: she had a gambling addiction. Arkwright is known to have lent her several thousand pounds for her gambling debts, which, true to form, she did not repay before requesting a further loan. Although by this point Arkwright had become concerned, he did not refuse her. In 1788, £1,000 was equivalent to over £120,000 at today's values. Sir Richard Arkwright died in 1792 but, around 1804 Richard Arkwright's son, also called Richard (1755–1843), became a partner in the Wirksworth and Ashbourne, Derbyshire Bank which had been established in 1780. Subsequently it had become known as Messrs Richard Arkwright and Company Bank, Wirksworth. Wirksworth is a Derbyshire village about 2 miles from Cromford and 12 miles from Chatsworth. The Duchess of Devonshire borrowed heavily from this bank as well and, again, repayment was a non-event. The Greyhound Inn (built 1788) in Cromford was used as a place for business transactions by the Arkwright family. It was here, in the public room used for their business, that Richard Arkwright Jnr instructed the Duchess of Devonshire to leave her proposals for repaying the money the bank had loaned her. Her gambling debts were legendary, and at one point she owed £60,000. She also had at least £40,000 of debts in France. The Duchess died in 1806, aged only 48. She had lost her looks, put on a great deal of weight and had become seriously ill. It was widely believed that both her illness and her early death were due to the stress of her gambling debts. It is unlikely that she ever repaid her huge debts in full, and, so far as is known, the debt she owed to the Arkwrights died with her. Despite their financial loss, neither Richard Arkwright Jnr nor his bank would have wanted to make an enemy of her husband, a very powerful and influential man, who had never been told the full extent of her debts and with whom any conflict would have been extremely inadvisable and injurious for their business.

Richard Arkwright had proved himself to be an able and very successful entrepreneur and businessman which is how he should be remembered. An inventor of machinery he was not. However, his self-promotion was such that, 230 years after his death, English history still teaches its students that Arkwright invented the water frame, and he was the father of the British factory system. That is simply not true.

Chapter 17

An English Postscript

Subsequently, in August 1823, an interesting witness statement came from a weaver named Thomas Leather who, as a child, had lived with his family for a while on a street named The Walk in Leigh. He stated that 'their next-door neighbour on the south side was Thomas Highs, reed maker, on the north side was John Kay, clock-maker.' He went on to say that while they were living there

> there was much talk amongst the neighbours about a spinning machine that Highs and Kay were making in Highs' garrett; that Highs and Kay worked at this machine during over hours, sometimes working until late at night; that after they had worked at it some months, they, one Sunday evening, threw or carried it into the back yard and broke it up, and on the Monday morning, he [Thomas Leather], took a wheel or pulley for a trundle bowl from the broken machine as it lay in the yard; and that when the neighbours heard that Highs and Kay had broken the machine they laughed at them. Kay said he would have no more to do with spinning machines. Highs, however, was not satisfied, but took the broken machine into his garret and soon after completed a spinning jenny. The jenny made by Highs had six spindles which stood at the front of the jenny and were turned by strings from a drum working on a perpendicular axle; and that the clove [two pieces of wood to hold rovings, long narrow bundles of

fibre, securely] worked perpendicularly, 'rising when drawing put the weft, and falling when it was copped'. After Highs had invented this machine he did not work much at reed making, but was employed in making and scheming machines for spinning. John Kay left Leigh, going to live at Warrington about the time [Thomas Leather] moved from their house in The Walk, and that Thomas Highs and his family went to live in a house in Bradshaw-gate in Leigh, about the same time.

It was an interesting confirmation that Highs and Kay had once enjoyed a working partnership inventing a spinning machine.

Chapter 18

An Italian Postscript

Giovanni Battista Mazioni

On the top floor of the Museo del Tessuto di Prato, there is a small bust of an Italian gentleman named as Giovani Battista Mazioni. He represented everything which the Italians could have wished for in karma and poetic justice after the John Lombe affair. Giovani Battista Mazioni was born at Prato in 1789. He subsequently studied at the University of Pisa, about 50 miles (81km) from Prato, whose records contain the only known mention of John Lombe in the Italian archives. Afterwards he took apprenticeships in Paris and Rouen, and while in France he extensively studied the mechanisms of the French cotton textile manufacturing machinery. The French had bought the latest in cotton-manufacturing machinery from England and it was expressly forbidden to copy any part of it. The Greek historian Thucydides stated that 'history is cyclical' and history obliged this assertion by now repeating itself with great irony.

Giovani had been blessed with a photographic memory. As an apprentice he studied the machines very carefully, but he took no notes, and he made no drawings. He simply memorised their construction. On his return to Italy, he rebuilt the machines he had studied in France quite accurately from memory, completing his work in 1819. As the silk-throwing machinery of medieval Italy, which became a blueprint for the water frame, had been 'improved' by men like Leonardo da Vinci, Taccola and Martini, so men like Thomas Highs and John Kay had further 'improved' this machinery which was again 'improved' by others like Samuel Crompton, and

147

possibly even by Mazioni himself. Giovanni Mazioni went on to build the first cotton mill in Italy at Prato which began production in 1822, 100 years after John Lombe's death. The cotton industry in Italy grew rapidly and by the time of his death in 1867, Giovani Battista Mazioni had become a very wealthy and respected man; and the Italians had their revenge for John Lombe's espionage. By the reception desk of the Museo del Tessuto there is a photograph of closely packed cotton mills with tall smoking chimneys which, the inscription informs, was taken in 1890. On my commenting that the image was just like Manchester, the Italian receptionist misunderstood and hastened to correct what she believed was a wrong impression. 'No, no!' she said. 'Is not Manchester. Is Prato!'

Epilogue

Industrial technology goes much further back than most people realise. It is as though there was a gap between Antiquity and the modern day during which nothing much happened, but that is far from the truth. Ways of doing things more easily and quickly have always been attractive and, after the plagues of the Black Death, became essential when physical people power was much reduced. Conversely there has been suspicion and resistance to 'new-fangled ways and means' which create fear that jobs and livelihoods will be lost as a result. Progress can be a double-edged sword as the Emperor Vespasian discovered in the decades after Christ's death (p.9), but life and inventions go on as they always have done throughout the centuries.

The natural energy forms of sun, wind and water have long been harnessed as sources of power. According to the Renewable Energy Hub, solar energy has been used since the seventh century BC, while the Greeks and Romans used 'burning mirrors' to light ceremonial torches, a method copied by the Chinese in the first century AD. Meanwhile, according to various historians, wind power is known to have been harnessed to sail boats along the Nile by the Egyptians as early as 5000 BC, and subsequently by the Phoenicians, during their empire-building voyages 1500–300 BC, and the feared 'Sea Peoples' who destroyed the Mycenean and Minoan civilisations around 1200 BC. Windmills, utilising wind as a power source, are said to have originally been the idea of Hammurabi, a Babylonian ruler, in 1700 BC, but in the couple of centuries before Christ's birth, it was a Greek engineer, Heron of Alexandria, who first put the principle into practice. Windmills were in use in China around the same time, but the 'modern' windmill originated in Persia (now Iran) during the eighth and ninth centuries AD. The power of falling water was recognised far back in pre-history and the Greeks of Antiquity (*c.*3000 BC–AD 400) utilised water to turn wheels which provided the power used for milling and grinding, although the first written reference, by Philo of Byzantium, comes from around 250 BC. By comparison, coal, gas and oil are 'Johnny-come-lately' forms of energy which have caused great ecological damage to the extent that solar, wind and water power are once more being promoted as chief sources of power. It is generally agreed among industrial historians that, in fact, Italy was the leading technological power in Europe until at least the seventeenth century. Both wind- and water power were widely used in Italy, although water power was favoured because it was not so dependent upon the weather. During medieval times and the Renaissance, Britain had not been at the forefront of the cutting edge in technology and was sometimes slow to adopt new ideas. Over fifty years after John Lombe's success with his water-powered factory and machinery, Richard Arkwright initially persisted in using horsepower at both his Nottingham and Cromford mills before finally realising that water power was far cheaper and more efficient.

Patents, the cause of so much trouble in eighteenth-century England, seem to have originated in Italy during the fifteenth century. Ironically, the first recorded patent was granted by Florence in 1421 to Filippo Brunelleschi, the engineer responsible for building the dome of Florence cathedral. The first English patent was granted in 1449 by Henry IV to John of Utynam, an immigrant Flemish stained-glass maker, for a new process of making glass. His products were then used for the windows of Eton College. Patents proved to be another double-edged sword. While they protected inventions and trades, they granted patentees monopolies in manufactures and sales of commodities. In Italy, although patents and products were jealously guarded by the country as a whole for its own benefit, there appeared to be an accepted practice whereby the engineers and inventors of each generation could 'improve' upon the work and designs of their predecessors without piles of paperwork and new patents. That did not seem to be the case in England as the stories of the Lombes and Richard Arkwright demonstrate. The inventions, methods and manufacture were not shared but were kept closely guarded by the patentees in case they should be stolen, which could damage future potential profits. The supreme irony in this story is that the machines involved were not the inventions of the patentees who were simply using the law to prevent anyone else from doing what they had done themselves. In fact, Arkwright was paranoid about having 'his inventions stolen from him', which was the raison d'être for his numerous court cases, although it was conclusively proved that they were never his inventions in the first place.

Karma, however, works in mysterious ways. Despite his treachery towards the Italians and his untimely death, John Lombe had introduced the concept of water-powered machinery and factories to England in 1719 as a means of producing fine silk effectively and efficiently, challenging both the Italian and French silk trades, but, despite his efforts, silk production had begun to decline in keeping with changes of fashion during the 1760s. By the 1770s, it was becoming very clear that the manufacture and production of cotton materials was going to be the way forward. As a result, the silk industry was overtaken, and almost obliterated at one point, by Cottonopolis (the name given to Manchester and its locality where cotton mills were prevalent in large numbers). In Italy, the textile industry, especially that of silk, had blossomed much earlier. Silk had become a major industry in Italy during later medieval times, surviving the turbulent political centuries which followed, but still maintaining its special qualities, so that even in the twenty-first century Italian silk is still regarded as a great luxury. Nevertheless, the English silk industry fought back doggedly and began to grow and prosper once more throughout the nineteenth and twentieth centuries. It was helped by renewed demands for luxury garments throughout late Victorian and Edwardian England, and again during the 1920s. The Second World War helped as well in that silk is lighter, stronger and thinner than canvas for use in parachutes, and it also proved to be ideal for wound dressings and sutures.

This book has been an attempt to put the record straight and to acknowledge the part that Italy has played in the development of modern textile technology in Britain, a country long renowned for its woollens and linens, and only comparatively latterly for silks and cottons. There are no complete working models of the silk-throwing machinery built by John Lombe left in Britain. The silk mill itself suffered a couple of disastrously destructive fires during the nineteenth century from which virtually nothing has survived, and, although other models were built after parliament had refused to renew Thomas Lombe's patent, little remains. The Museum of Science and Industry in Manchester holds much of what is left, but this only includes remnants of the original silk-throwing machinery that had proved to be the blueprint for the later cotton-spinning machinery.

Thucydides, an eminent Greek historian of the fifth century BC, wisely prophesied that history is cyclical, and this still seems to be the case 2,500 years later. The British silk industry has survived, but greatly helped through the production of a variety of utilitarian silk goods as well as lingerie and luxury items, and in the twenty-first century a new 'cottage industry' of silk painting has grown in Britain whereby skilled artists paint colourful designs on to Italian silks. The Silk Association of Great Britain currently states that 'the UK silk industry exports millions of pounds of goods throughout the world' which include medical suture supplies, knitted silk gloves for fighter jet pilots and fabrics for interior furnishings as well as the more traditional use for garments; but it seems that fashions have largely remained the provenance of Italy. Someone once commented that the luxury, quality and feel of silk is so special and unique there will always be a market for the fabric because of its soft sensual touch against the skin.

Cotton has not fared so well. Despite the huge manufacturing base of cotton in the north-west, the cotton industry was eclipsed by a number of factors including widespread selling of cotton-manufacturing machinery to other countries and failing to source alternative supplies of cotton during and after the American Civil War (1861–1865). Cotton was a latecomer to the scene of textile industries and less than a century after Cottonopolis had begun, the American Civil War was to mark the beginning of the end for the British cotton industry. This was followed by the disastrous decision to sell British cotton-manufacturing machinery abroad during the 1880s/1890s which enabled other nations, including America, India, and Japan, to start up their own cotton-manufacturing businesses and undercut British prices. For India, revenge for the ruination of their own cotton industry by the British East India Company must have seemed infinitely sweet. After a brief resurgence during the First World War, the coffin of the British cotton industry was finally firmly nailed down during the 1920s when Japan instigated twenty-four-hour working in its cotton manufactories, meeting deadlines that were impossible for the British cotton industry to meet, and by a renewed preference by the public for the cheaper and more colourful cottons produced by India. The cotton industry struggled to try and make a comeback with a series of initiatives, like the Cotton Queens of the 1930s, but failed. The invention of nylon, the world's first synthetic fabric, in the 1930s, followed by polyester and acrylic, which were cheaper and easier to care for than cotton, precipitated the end of the cotton industry. Many mills were demolished. Some were utilised for housing apartments. Helmshore Mill and Queen Street Mill in Burnley became museums. Quarry Bank Mill at Styal in Cheshire became a working mill so that future generations could see and understand what living and working in the millscapes had meant for so many unknown, nameless and forgotten mill workers. However, history continues to be cyclical and, in a twenty-first-century postscript, English Fine Cottons has restored the Tower Mill on Park Road in Dukinfield (now a township of Tameside in Great Manchester) for commercial production. The company describes itself as 'the only commercial cotton spinner in the UK' which has 'a state-of-the-art cotton-spinning facility – the first to be established in the UK for more than fifty years'.

There are many inventions from the Industrial Revolution of which the British can be justly proud, but the inventions of the water frame and the factory system are not among them. There was no single inventor, more an evolution of inventors and inventions coming together over the years. Italian archive records clearly show the use of wind- and water power for a number of industrial activities, including silk throwing, and the establishment of a factory system centuries before John Lombe copied them and introduced them to Britain over fifty years before Richard Arkwright built Cromford Mill. Shared knowledge is important, although it is not always willingly given. Richard Arkwright was guilty of industrial espionage as much as John Lombe, the main difference being that he committed that espionage in his own country rather than in someone else's. Italy was, without doubt, one of the leading contributors in the field of textile manufacturing machinery, until the eighteenth century, and the time has come to acknowledge their contribution. There is no dishonour in recording that the water frame and the factory system were due to Italian invention and initiatives. Now the British educational system must admit the part played by Italian inventors and engineers in the Industrial Revolution and cease issuing history curricula which repeat the falsehood that Richard Arkwright was 'the father of the Industrial Revolution and of the factory system'. Both he and the Lombes were skilled entrepreneurs, who were not averse to 'borrowing' other people's ideas, but they were not original inventors. It is time to set the record straight.

Bibliography

Aiken, John. *A Description of the Countryside from Thirty to Forty Miles around Manchester*. (1795)

Arkwright, Richard. *A case for the consideration of Parliament*, relative to his invention of an Engine for spinning Cotton into Yarn (printed in 1782. Republished in: House of Commons (1829) *Report from the Select Committee on the Law Relative to Patents for Inventions*

Baines, Edward. *History of the Cotton Manufacture in Great Britain* (Fisher, Fisher and Jackson. 1835).

Beck, S. William. *The Draper's Dictionary: A Manual of Textile Fabrics, Their History and Applications.* (London. 1882)

Bertucci, Paola. 'Enlightened Secrets: Silk, 4, Intelligent Travel and Industrial Espionage in Eighteenth-Century France'. (*Technology and Culture*, Volume 54, no 4, October 2013, pp. 820–52)

Bolts, William. *Consideration of Indian Affairs*. (1772)

Calladine, A. *Lombe's Mill*. p.97 (1993)

Century France. (*Technology and Culture* Volume 54 no 4, October 2013)

Cianchi, Marco. *Leonardo da Vinci's Machines* (Becocci Editore, 1988)

Cipolla, Carlos M. *Before the Industrial Revolution*. (Methuen, 1976)

Comino, Stefano, and Gasparetto, 'Alessandra. Silk Mills in Early Modern Italy'. (*Advances in Historical Studies,* 9, 284–94. 2020)

Encyclopædia Britannica 1801, 1803; Supplement to the Encyclopaedia cited by Guest [1823])

Goldthwaite, Richard A. *The Economy of Renaissance Florence.* (JHU Press. 2009)

Guest, Richard. *A Compendious History of the Cotton-manufacture: with a Disproval of the Claim of Sir Richard Arkwright to the Invention of Its Ingenious Machinery of Sir Richard Arkwright to the invention of its ingenious machinery.* (J. Pratt, 1823)

Hansard 1719

Hare, J.C. *Guesses at Truth.* (Plumptree, 1871)

Hooper, Luther. *Silk, its production and manufacture.* (Pitman. 1919)

Hutton, William. *History of Derby.* (1791)

Journals of the House of Commons (Volume 21 for 1731 reprinted 1803)

Lombe, Thomas. *Engines to Wind, Spin and Twist Silk.* (Lombe's Patent No 422. AD1718)

Oxford Dictionary of National Biography (OUP 2004)

Polo, Marco. *Marco Polo's Silk Road.* (Watkins Publishing, 2011)

Poni, Carlo. *La Seta in Italia.* (2009)

Smiles, Samuel. *Men of invention and industry.* (J. Murray. 1890)

Taglialagamba, Sara. *Leonardo and Engineering.* (CB Publishers, 2011)

'The English Silk Industry in the Eighteenth Century'. (*English Historical Review*, 1909)

Usher, Abbott Payson. *A History of Mechanical Inventions.* (Dover Publications, 1929)

Warner, Frank. *The Silk Industry.* (Dianes, London. 1921)

Wills, Matthew. *Eighteenth-Century Spies in the European Silk Industry.* (daily.jstor.org 2021)

Wood, Michael. *The History of China.* (Simon & Schuster. 2020)

Zonca, Vittorio di. *Novo Teatro di Machine et Edificii per Uarie et Sicure Operationi.* (Italy, 1607)

Institutions

Bodleian Library, Oxford
Derby Silk Mill
Helmshore Mills Burnley
Leonardian Library of Vinci
Leonardo Museum, Castle of Vinci
Museo della Storia di Scienza, Florence
Museo del Tessuto, Prato
Museum of Science and Industry Manchester
National State Library of Florence

Timeline

5000 BC	Silkworms first cultivated in eastern China
3000 BC	Silk production began as a cottage industry along Yellow River in Henan Province
c. **3000** BC	Silk Road trading route established within Chinese borders
c. **200** BC	Silk Road begins to extend beyond Chinese borders
c. **100** BC	Reeling machines and flyers for twisting and doubling in use in China
476	Roman Empire collapses and Italy enters a 'Dark Age' recession
c. **500**	Byzantine silk farms established in Greece and Syria
c. **600**	Persia invents first windmills
711	Moorish invasion of southern Europe begins but silk manufacture continues
c. **750**	Arab silk farms established in Sicily and Spain
1056	Calabria in southern Italy has cultivated 24,000 mulberry trees for silkworms
c. **1090**	Chinese invent machine for unwinding silkworm cocoons

Timeline

c. **1090**	Cantazaro is first Italian city to introduce silk production
1095–1099	First Crusade
1147–1149	Second Crusade
1184–1192	Third Crusade
1202–1204	Fourth Crusade
c. **1210**	Silk reeling machinery and flyers adopted in Europe
c. **1210**	First records of spinning wheel in Europe. Chinese claims of superior looms
1221	Silk doubling machines in use in Italy
1250	Italian Renaissance begins
1260	Italian traders Niccolo and Maffeo Polo travel to China to the court of Kublai Khan
1270–1280	Silk doubling machines perfected in Bologna
1271	Marco Polo travels with his father and uncle when they return to China
1271	Marco Polo writes *Silk Road*
1295	Polo family return to Italy following silk trade routes
1300s	Improvements to reeling and silk throwing in Italy
1313	First silk-spinning machine powered by water in Europe
1313–1315	Great Famine kills 15 per cent of European population

1331	Twisting mill built in Lucca
1331	Flemish silk weavers first brought to England by Edward III
1347–1349	Black Death kills up to 60 per cent of European population
1349	Boccaccio writes The Decameron and describes effects of plague in Italy
1350	Water-powered silk-manufacturing mill built in Bologna by Bolognino di Borghesano
1352	Italian engineer Mariano Taccola born
1363	First reference to silk weaving in English statute books
1439	Italian engineer and scientist Francesco Martini born
1452	Polymath Leonardo da Vinci born
1455	English 'silk women and spinsters of silk' given legal protection against imports
1472	Eighty-four silk workshops and 7,000 silk craftsmen in Florence
1519	Catanzaro establishes silk craft consulate
1521	France begins silk manufacture
1564	Galileo Galilei born
1568	Vittorio di Zonca born
1598	Edict of Nantes

Timeline

1600	East India Company incorporated
1607	Di Zonca's book on engineering and building published for the first time
1620	'Broad silk' manufacture introduced to England
1629	Silk Throwsters Company established in London
1661	40,000 employed by Silk Throwsters Company
1665	Great Fire of London
1666	Black Death arrives in Eyam in bales of cloth
1685	Revocation of the Edict of Nantes
1685	Thomas Lombe born
1686	Henry Lombe born
1680	Dutch manufacture silk-throwing machinery
1680s	Genoese and Piedmont silk industry begins to decline
1692	Royal Lustrings Company incorporates Spitalfields silk spinners
1693	John Lombe born
1703	Thomas Cotchett builds first silk mill in Derby
***c.* 1705**	John Lombe employed by Cotchett's mill
1713	Cotchett's mill fails
1714–1715	John Lombe hatches plot for industrial espionage to steal Italian silk machinery plans
1716	John Lombe arrives in Italy

1717	George Sorocold commissioned to build Derby Silk Mill
1717–1719	John Lombe reconstructs Italian silk-throwing machinery from stolen plans
1718	Thomas Lombe obtains fourteen-year patent for 'new machinery'
1719	Derby Silk Mill open for business
1720	South Sea Bubble bursts
1722	John Lombe dies. Foul play is suspected
1727	Thomas Lombe receives knighthood and is elected Sheriff of London
1732	Thomas Lombe loses his patent on the Italian originated silk-throwing machinery
1732	Richard Arkwright born
1738	Lewis Paul and John Wyatt invent roller system and flyer/bobbin system
1760s	Cotton is gaining in popularity over silk which is beginning to decline
1763	Smuggling of silk from France also causing problems for English silk workers
1763	Thomas Highs/John Kay invent a spinning machine on which water frame was based
1767	Arkwright and Kay meet and form a partnership
1768	Arkwright patents water frame without telling Kay
1771	Arkwright builds Cromford Mill near Matlock in Derbyshire

1773	Will Hutton, worker and recorder of life in Derby Silk Mill, born
1774	Dr Johnson visits Derby Silk Mill
1781	First court cases against Richard Arkwright for plagiarism
1782	Arkwright loses his cases for being unable to sketch machine he said he invented
1785	final court case against Richard Arkwright and he loses his patents
1785	cotton has been largely substituted for silk in fashions and furnishings
1792	Sir Richard Arkwright dies a rich and successful man
1821	Richard Guest writes a book stating why Arkwright lost his cases of plagiarism
1822	Italians open first cotton manufactory in Italy at Prato, a Florence township
1861–1865	American Civil War signals beginning of the end for the cotton industry
1871	Unification of Italy
1920s	British cotton industry in great decline as unable to compete against Japan, India and USA
1940s	Silk industry enjoys revival boost as it is used for parachutes and surgical dressings
2000s	British silk industry has flourished and exports bring in millions of pounds each year
2000s	British cotton industry has greatly declined although there is some revival by 2019

Acknowledgement and thanks are due to the following institutions and individuals for all their help:

    Bodleian Library, Oxford
    Derby Silk Mill
    Derbyshire County Council Picture the Past
    Forgotten Books publishers
    Helmshore Mills Burnley
    Leonardian Library of Vinci
    Leonardo Museum, Castle of Vinci
    Manchester Central Library Local Studies Archives
    Museo della Storia di Scienza, Florence
    Museo del Tessuto, Prato
    Museum of Science and Industry Manchester
    National State Library of Florence

and to Michael Wood for information on early Chinese trade routes; Simona Continente for help with the translation of Italian to English; the editorial staff of Pen & Sword for suggestions and guidance; to family and friends for patience and proofreading.

Index